07/08

UNIVERSITY OF
WOLVERHAMPTON

Walsall Learning Centre
University of Wolverhampton
Gorway Road
Walsall WS1 3BD
Telephone: 0845 408 1631
Online Renewals:
www.wlv.ac.uk/lib/myaccount

Telephone Renewals: 01902 321333 or 0845 408 1631
Please Return this item on or before the last date shown above.
Fines will be charged if items are returned late.
See tariff of fines displayed at the Counter.

Teaching Number Sense

Julia Anghileri

Continuum

London and New York

Continuum

Wellington House
125 Strand
London WC2R 0BB

370 Lexington Avenue
New York
NY 10017–6503

First published 2000

British Library Cataloguing-in-Publication Data
A catalogue record for this book is available from the British Library.

ISBN 0-8264-4819-4 (hb)
    0-8264-4807-0 (pb)

Typeset by YHt Ltd, London
Printed and bound in Great Britain by The Cromwell Press Ltd, Trowbridge, Wiltshire

Contents

List of Figures

List of Figures

For Ellie and Evie

CHAPTER 1

Making Sense of Numbers

Every teacher can sympathize with the frustration felt by a child who cannot solve apparently straightforward and simple arithmetic problems. As soon as symbols are introduced there are children who become confused and unsure, often despite considerable effort on their own and their teacher's part. When older children struggle to solve ? $- 4 = 9$ or $100 \div 25 = ?$ instead of *recognizing* the number relations involved, it is probable that they are seeking to identify an appropriate *procedure* to solve the problem while other children are able to use facts that they already know. It is not only effort that gives some children a facility with numbers, but an awareness of relationships that enables them to interpret new problems in terms of results that they remember. Children who have this awareness and the ability to work flexibly to solve number problems are said to have a 'feel' for numbers or 'number sense'. What characterizes children with 'number sense' is their ability to make generalizations about the patterns and processes that they have met, and to link new information to their existing knowledge. How to teach the connections involved in developing number sense will be the central focus of this book, which will highlight the key ideas at each stage in children's learning.

Number sense and the school curriculum

In the past, 'arithmetic' has meant multiplication tables and the four rules of number (that is, the concise methods of performing written addition, subtraction, multiplication and division). The meaning of 'arithmetic' has over time become limited to perform-ance in standard algorithms without an underlying understanding. In society today there is general acceptance that 'drill and practice' of taught routines will not prepare children for life in a techno-logical society and that teaching approaches need to focus on the links that demonstrate the logical structure underlying numbers and number operations. Rather than being shown how to do written calculations, children are to be encouraged to work mentally, to observe patterns, to predict results and to talk about the connections that can be made.

Reform of the mathematics curriculum has led to a shift from teaching standard procedures for calculating, to enabling children to observe patterns and relationships, and make connections so that they develop insight and a 'feel' for numbers. The Cockcroft report used the phrase 'at-homeness with numbers' to describe one of the desirable attributes of a 'numerate adult' (Cockcroft, 1982, p. 39). More recently, the UK *Framework for Teaching Mathematics from Reception to Year 6* (DfEE, 1999) uses the term 'numeracy' to identify 'the proficiency in number that involves a confidence and competence with numbers requiring an understanding of the number system, a repertoire of computational skills and an inclination and ability to solve number problems in a variety of contexts' (DfEE, 1998). 'Numeracy' goes beyond the requirement of teaching written calculating procedures to involve both mental calculation and estimation as efficient processes for calculating. There are increased roles for oral work, for 'choosing' appropriate strategies, and for reflecting on and explaining both the processes and the results of any calculation.

Curriculum reforms are widespread throughout the world and typified by the United States *Curriculum and Evaluation Standards for School Mathematics* (NCTM, 1989), and *National Statement for Australian Schools* (AEC, 1991) where the identification of 'number sense' is a major essential outcome of the school curriculum. This 'number sense', which is widely used in reform documents, refers to 'flexibility' and 'inventiveness' in strategies for calculating and is a reaction to overemphasis on computational procedures devoid of thinking. It refers not only to the development of understanding but also to the nurturing of a positive attitude and confidence that have been lacking in more dated curricula.

The beginnings of number sense

By watching, listening and copying, children will initially learn isolated facts, but from the earliest stages they can be encouraged to see different ways that numbers are used and the connections that underlie their use. The number 6, for example, will not only be known as the name associated with a set of six objects, but also as the number after 5 and before 7, and 6 may also be recognized as a pattern of '2 and 2 and 2' or '4 and 2' or 'double 3'. As their experiences of individual numbers progress, children can quickly become aware of how each number can be related to many others.

Early experiences with number operations will also provide important links across many structures that underpin children's understanding. Adding one more to a collection, for example, does not mean that the whole collection needs to be re-counted as the next number word in the counting sequence gives the new total. Similarly, taking one away gives the previous counting number. In this way, connections are established between addition, subtraction and counting, with links that will form the foundations for effective calculating strategies that will be discussed in later chapters.

Number sense is highly personalized and relates not only to those ideas about number that have been established but also to how these have been established. It involves a way of thinking that enables children to identify quickly important relationships, such as recognizing that '$32 \div 16$' will prove to be significantly less problematic than '$32 \div 17$', or that '$47 - 38$' is effectively calculated by 'adding on to 38'. It also involves the ability to work flexibly with numbers and operations, for example knowing not only that '48' is '$40 + 8$', but also that it is '$50 - 2$' and 'double 24', and that '$8 \times \frac{1}{4}$' is not only '8 lots of $\frac{1}{4}$' but also '$8 \div 4$'. The way numbers relate to each other, the possibilities for different representations and the meanings that can be associated with different operations will all play a key role in establishing the connections that are crucial in developing number sense.

The goals in teaching number sense

The skills and understanding needed in preparation for living in the twenty-first century revolve around the recognition of patterns and relationships that are central to effective working with numbers. There is an expectation that individuals will use their initiative in making connections between real life problems and appropriate mathematical representation and that they will respond flexibly in finding appropriate ways to tackle them.

Number sense ... reflects an inclination and an ability to use numbers and quantitative methods as a means of communicating, processing and interpreting information. It results in an expectation that mathematics has a certain regularity.

(Mcintosh *et al.*, 1992, p. 3)

Today assessment tasks have also been developed to match the changing requirements. They are no longer stereotypical numerical calculations that require standard written procedures for calculating. Children are expected to extract information from charts and tables, to calculate with missing digits and to investigate number patterns where asking appropriate questions will help to identify numerical relationships. They are expected to make choices about the most appropriate procedures including the decision whether or not to use a calculator. These ideas mark a new departure for mathematics so that isolated procedures for calculating are not adequate and teaching children to make connections has become a crucial requirement.

How is number sense developed?

From the earliest stages of learning about numbers, children can be making connections that will establish a flexibility in their thinking that is characteristic in developing number sense. Some links between numbers are established through patterns in counting and the following chapters will show how teaching children about counting is an important preparation for calculating. 'Counting' here does not mean only the 'unitary' counting in ones that is a child's first experience, but includes counting in 2s, 5s, 10s and 100s, starting with any number and moving forwards and backwards. The patterns of numbers established in such counting can encourage the development of strategies that are powerful when they are connected to the arithmetic operations.

There are also connections to be established among the operations and links to be made with the particular numbers that appear in problems. If the reader takes time to do the three calculations: $25 + 26$, $39 + 17$ and $12 + 35$, it will probably become clear that a different strategy is used for each one, using results and relationships that are relevant. The first may be derived quickly from the 'known fact' that $25 + 25 = 50$. The second may be 'transformed' to $40 + 16 = 56$ while the third is most likely to involve 'partition-ing' the numbers to find $10 + 30 + 2 + 5$, or some similar procedure. Applying a standard procedure would not be as effi-cient as this selection of appropriate strategies based on number sense.

> Number sense refers to a person's general understanding of number and operations along with the ability and inclination to use this under-standing in flexible ways to make mathematical judgements and to develop useful strategies for handling numbers and operations.
>
> (Mcintosh *et al.*, 1992, p. 3)

According to the analysis of Mcintosh *et al.* (1992) there are three key areas where number sense plays a key role:

- *knowledge of and facility with numbers* – a sense of orderliness of number; multiple representations for numbers; a sense of relative and absolute magnitude of numbers; and a system of benchmark referents for thinking about numbers;
- *knowledge of and facility with operations* – an understanding of the effects of operations; an awareness of the rules that apply; and an awareness of the relationships between the operations;
- *applying this knowledge and facility with numbers and operations to problems requiring reasoning with numbers* – understanding the relationship between a problem context and appropriate solution strategies; awareness that multiple strategies exist; inclination to utilize an efficient representation and/or method; and an inclination to review data and results.

Knowledge of numbers involves an understanding of the structure and regularity of the number system, starting with whole numbers and extending to rational numbers (that is, those that can be represented as fractions and decimals) and the way these systems are linked. Facility with operations involves the links among them, for example doubling being the same as multiplying by 2. It includes an appreciation of certain rules and knowledge of when these can be used, for example in addition and multiplication the numbers can be reversed so that $8 + 3$ is equal to $3 + 8$ and 8×3 is equal to 3×8. For subtraction and division, on the other hand, reversing the numbers will give different calculations with different solutions. Utilizing numerical knowledge involves an understand-ing of which operations to use in problem-solving, knowing when it is appropriate to work with approximations and making sense of calculation procedures and results in terms of the original problem.

Some relationships are the crucial building blocks for working with numbers and these may be identified as 'benchmarks', for example the number pairs that make 10, or the equivalence of 0.5, ½ and 50%. When presented with a new problem, whether it is in words or symbols, an effective solution strategy will involve careful consideration of the numbers involved to identify links with any facts or relationships that are already known. Number sense develops continually as the range of known facts and the relationships among them are extended. But how are inexperienced children to come to know which facts are crucial to *know* and which are easily *derived* from others? It is here that judgement differs from one individual to another and the gap in apparent ability begins to open. What has been termed the 'seven-year gap' in children's mathematical ability becomes evident by the top of the primary school with some eleven year olds performing no better than average seven year olds while others show the ability of average fourteen year olds (Cockcroft, 1982, p. 342). It has been suggested that the term 'slow learner' with respect to mathematics is a misnomer as children who are struggling are often not identifying links and relationships and are consequently learning more, unconnected procedures (Gray and Tall, 1994, p. 135). The example used is the child who sees no connection between addition, subtraction and counting and so has three unrelated processes to master. Learning that subtraction can be achieved by counting on from the smaller number is one of the 'benchmarks' in early calculating.

The importance of understanding

'Understanding relationships between numbers and developing methods of computation' has become the focus for learning, replacing the traditional 'four rules of arithmetic' in curriculum requirements. Although the number facts to be acquired are often the same as in the past, the process of learning now involves children in constructing their own methods. Guidance from teachers will help them to develop efficiency without loss of understanding (*Mathematics in the National Curriculum*, DFE, 1995, p. 7). Work of eminent psychologists has led teachers to recognize the need to involve pupils actively in their own learning and to focus on mathematics as a thinking process rather than a catalogue of facts and procedures to memorize. This is reflected in the shift from endless 'drill and practice' of standard procedures, that was typical for past generations, to *using* mathematics, *communicating* mathematically and developing mathematical *reasoning*. Children are no longer considered as 'passive' receivers of information, but are 'actively' involved in constructing their own knowledge through discussing their own strategies and making sense of those used by others. Explaining what they are doing and justifying their decisions helps children to develop skills in reasoning and clarity in communication that will have benefits across many aspects of learning. Such developments in teaching, all of which have learning with understanding as a central requirement, reflect the views of psychologists and researchers about the most effective ways to help children learn mathematics.

A key objective for teaching is to establish learning with understanding. Understanding, however, is not easy to define and two different types of understanding have been identified with respect to mathematics. The type of understanding required to reproduce taught procedures has been called '*instrumental understanding*' and compared with '*relational understanding*' where knowledge extends from *how* to do a calculation to *why* the procedures work (Skemp, 1976). While number work in the past has been associated with tedious repetition of standard procedures, more recent trends in teaching have introduced investigational approaches and a classroom environment where the thinking of individuals is valued. For 'relational' understanding, learners are never asked to accept but instead are asked to try developing their own meanings. Skemp proposes that 'relational knowledge can be a goal in itself for if people get satisfaction from relational understanding they may not only try to understand relationally new material which is put before them, but also actively seek out new material and explore new areas ... making what is often called the "motivational side" of a teacher's job much easier' (Skemp, 1976).

Developing mental imagery

Mathematical understanding involves progression from practical experiences to talking about these experiences, first using informal language, and then more formal language. Later children will learn to use the symbols that characterize the conciseness and precision of a mathematically reasoned argument. Just as speech is transferred to writing over an extended period of time in school, with complexities arising in manipulative control and spelling, so transfer from concrete experiences to mental methods and symbolic representation takes time in mathematics.

$$\begin{bmatrix} \text{concrete} \\ \text{experiences} \end{bmatrix} \rightarrow \begin{bmatrix} \text{abstract/mental} \\ \text{methods} \end{bmatrix} \rightarrow \begin{bmatrix} \text{symbolizing} \\ \text{relations} \end{bmatrix}$$

Beginning with the manipulation of real objects, sorting and re-arranging different collections, children are introduced to patterns that will be identified with number words. The number '3', for example, can be represented as a collection of three buttons, or as three toys or three steps, but '3' itself is an abstraction from each of these situations. Talking about their experiences will help children establish the significance of number words that relate to the visual patterns that they consistently meet and provide the foundations for mental imagery.

Mental imagery can also be encouraged through patterns and symbols. Sometimes patterns are more evident in written form than in the spoken words, for example starting with 13 and adding tens will result in the pattern '13, 23, 33, 43, 53, 63 ...'. Here the counting pattern '1, 2, 3. ...' appears in the first 'place' for each number and will continue '93, 103, 113 ... ', although the words to be matched to these higher numbers give less of a clue that this pattern continues. Making patterns explicit and building connections between different visual images will help to establish relationships that exist among numbers.

Before they can operate with abstract numbers, children will learn to 'model' situations with their fingers or some form of apparatus that can represent the real objects. In the classroom, beads or cubes are introduced because they can be linked together and so have the potential to represent numbers in a structured way. Cubes are sometimes favoured because they can be used not only to

Figure 1.1 (a) Cubes to show 'tens' and 'units'.
(b) A bead frame and a bead string.

model different numbers, but also to show the place value structure of the number system in 'tens' and 'units' (Figure 1.1a). An alternative representation of numbers that relates more closely to the counting sequence involves beads that can be joined on a 'bead frame' or in a 'bead string' (Figure 1.1b). 'Place value' and 'counting' will be seen in the chapters of this book as alternative focuses for early work with numbers, each identified with the development of different calculating strategies.

It is important that children do not come to rely on using such materials for modelling numbers but that they develop mental imagery associated with these materials and can work with 'imagined' situations. Research has shown that an important stage between the actual manipulation of objects and abstract work with numbers is a stage in which objects are imagined (Hughes, 1986). Although some children will progress spontaneously to using mental imagery, others may need a transitional stage in which the materials to be manipulated are covered or hidden once they have been used and the children encouraged to reproduce in their minds the procedures involved.

Classroom materials provide powerful images, not only for representing individual numbers, but also for illustrating the way numbers are related in a logical structure. Representation to focus on the ordering of numbers may be seen in various versions of the *number line*, which models the counting sequence. Initially the number line may be represented by linking beads on a string, or with cubes that can be structured into a line that is sometimes referred to as a *number track* (Figure 1.2a). At this stage each item will represent a number in the counting sequence but later, number labels will be 'attached' to the divisions between each item so that the number 12, for example, is associated with twelve complete sections on a number line (Figure 1.2b). This number line appears on rulers and scales, and experiences with measuring instruments will help to reinforce the meaning of the calibrations. Most recently, an *empty number line* has been introduced for modelling mental calculations where the number order is preserved but the intervals are not marked. Without marked intervals, numbers can be represented in a flexible way using 'jumps' to illustrate the stages in a calculation (Figure 1.2c).

In traditional classrooms the place value aspect of numbers has been emphasized more than counting, with images relating to the 'tens stick' and 'unit cubes' and later with *Dienes materials* including 'hundreds blocks' and even 'thousands cubes'. Using these materials, the operations of addition and subtraction can been identified with procedures for moving around the concrete blocks and related to written recording. Using this imagery the 'tens stick'

Figure 1.2 (a) Number track.
(b) Calibrated number line.
(c) Empty number line.

represents at the same time '10 unit ones' and '1 unit ten'. Similarly, a single flat block is used to represent '1 hundred' with its equivalence to '10 tens' and '100 ones' evident in the size and structure of the materials.

When number symbols are familiar, their arrangement on a *100 square* (Figure 1.3a) will illustrate the regularity with which certain symbols appear, and the logical structure of the symbol patterns, even where the words do not clearly relate to their position (for example, eleven or twelve). An alternative representation showing number structure is presented in a *Gattegno chart* (Figure 1.3b) which focuses on the way larger numbers are constructed by identifying their constituent parts. Using the images presented in such a chart, the number symbols and the words to identify them can be brought together. Children can be encouraged to identify the representation of numbers such as 364 ('three hundred and sixty-

1	2	3	4	5	6	7	8	9	10
11	12	13	14	15	16	17	18	19	20
21	22	23	24	25	26	27	28	29	30
31	32	33	34	35	36	37	38	39	40
41	42	43	44	45	46	47	48	49	50
51	52	53	54	55	56	57	58	59	60
61	62	63	64	65	66	67	68	69	70
71	72	73	74	75	76	77	78	79	80
81	82	83	84	85	86	87	88	89	90
91	92	93	94	95	96	97	98	99	100

(a)

1	2	3	4	5	6	7	8	9
10	20	30	40	50	60	70	80	90
100	200	300	400	500	600	700	800	900
1 000	2 000	3 000	4 000	5 000	6 000	7 000	8 000	9 000
10 000	20 000	30 000	40 000	50 000	60 000	70 000	80 000	90 000
100 000	200 000	300 000	400 000	500 000	600 000	700 000	800 000	900 000

(b)

Figure 1.3 (a) 100 square.
(b) Gattegno chart.

four') with 300 ('three hundred') and 60 ('sixty') and 4 ('four'). The different images presented by the number line and a 100 square will be associated with patterns in counting and in place value respectively and will be influential in the mental calculating strategies that children learn. The development of strategies from such imagery, particularly for addition and subtraction, will be discussed in later chapters of this book.

Further classroom resources

One of the most effective ways to encourage mental work and classroom discussion is through the use of games and puzzles, inside and outside the classroom. These can present further images of numbers in different structured formats and can motivate children to tackle numerous calculations in their heads. Games can stimulate children to reflect on numerical relationships in a way that encourages them to seek results and relationships that will be advantageous in their game strategy. They will draw on all their experiences with numbers in order to make sense of every situation that arises in a manner that more formal work with numbers does not always encourage. In support of games, Parr (1994, p. 29) writes that 'a game can stimulate people to do willingly some quite demanding and not very attractive arithmetic'. He also notes that 'games can stimulate people to give repeated practice to skills of mental arithmetic and then do the whole thing again simply because they want to do better the second time around'. This support for games is endorsed by Hatch (1998, p. 32), who suggests that games 'improve mental skills through repetition', provide children with a sense of ownership through which they become autonomous in their thinking, and develop skills in asking as well as answering questions. She notes that 'when playing a game there is pressure to work mentally' and there is encouragement to develop flexibility as 'a game does not define the way in which a problem is to be solved'. As a classroom resource, games can present teachers with opportunities for listening to children − 'eavesdropping on playing games is an excellent way to assess their mental skills' − and also 'to identify misconceptions'. Unlike tests, the traditional method for reinforcing mental skills, games are less threatening. When playing games, children's thinking can be more transparent, particularly where they are encouraged to 'think aloud' and share their strategies with others.

Problem solving or exploring structure

If children are to appreciate number work as a pursuit that makes sense, in addition to having appropriate images, they must be clear about the reasons for calculating. Separate learning objectives may be appropriate for different activities with numbers. Anghileri (2000) suggests two distinct purposes for calculating: for solving individual problems and for exploring the structure of the number system. *Calculating for problem solving* may require a 'convergent' methodology where the main aim is to find and interpret the solution to a particular problem. This will differ from the more analytical, 'divergent' approaches that are used in *calculating for exploring structure*, where the purpose is to focus on many possible approaches to a calculation in order to highlight the mathematical relationships and processes that can be involved.

- In *calculating for problem solving*, only one approach will be necessary in order to find a solution and it may not always be appropriate to debate the most succinct written method. The focus will be on interpreting the information for a given problem, modelling the situation arithmetically, and applying the result to a real solution of the problem. Division provides a good example of the way this may involve mathematical thinking, even where a calculator is used. For the problem 'How many buses are needed to transport 532 people on 15-seater buses?', initial identification of the operation as division would lead to the answer 35.466667 on a calculator which would then need to be interpreted in terms of the number of buses needed.

- In addition to the solution of a particular problem, experiences of *calculating for exploring structure* may involve many different ways to tackle a single calculation and discussion to assess the effectiveness of different approaches. The purpose will be to identify links among numbers, and among the operations, which will help to develop children's understanding of number relationships. An example may involve possible ways to calculate $300 - 158$, and could include the relationship between addition and subtraction, and the use of 'near doubles'. Particular types of calculation may be formalized in a written record to make explicit the rules and relationships that underpin the different approaches that are possible.

These different purposes for calculating could be combined but children need to be aware of the objectives in a particular activity and separating them out may provide a clearer agenda for children's learning. Each purpose will strengthen the skills and understanding gained from the other, and the two should be seen as complementary rather than separate, just as reading and writing are related elements in learning language.

Purposes in teaching mathematics

Wider perspectives for teaching number are introduced when the purposes in teaching mathematics are reviewed more generally. In discussing some of the different purposes that have been identified, Huckstep (1999) includes such utilitarian justifications for teaching mathematics as providing 'a tool in everyday life' and 'a means of communication' but also identifies its 'usefulness in providing mental training' and 'as a means for empowering people'. The first of these may be satisfied by teaching standardized procedures for calculating but the others suggest that computational skills without number sense will provide a poor educational opportunity to children. The flexibility and inventiveness identified with number sense will become established only where children are aware of the power of pure mathematical reasoning. This power has been acknowledged within ancient civilizations but most recently has led to the development of a technology that has had profound effects on society with the invention of calculators and computers. These are testament to the power of mathematical thinking that has its roots in children's earliest calculations.

All children can derive satisfaction from this mathematical thinking as they observe patterns and relationships that present connections among numbers or procedures, and teachers will be aware of the positive motivation that personal 'discoveries' can nurture. Huckstep discusses mathematics 'as a source of aesthetic satisfaction and a form of entertainment'. This may be contested by adults who were subjected to 'drill and practice' where rules were learned without reason and a feeling of inadequacy was common among perhaps the majority of children in the classroom. He highlights mathematical thinking as 'one of the pinnacles of mankind's intellectual achievements' and this can be reflected in the pleasure that can be experienced by children who feel in control of their work with numbers.

Learning about numbers and number operations can provide opportunities to go beyond the utilitarian applications to explore patterns and relationships that can be fascinating and can lead to logical thinking and mathematical reasoning. Observation based on simple calculations can, for example, lead to predictions and justifications that illustrate the way powerful thought may be initiated. Consider the fact that when the consecutive odd numbers are added the result is a square number:

$$1 + 3 = 2 \times 2$$
$$1 + 3 + 5 = 3 \times 3$$
$$1 + 3 + 5 + 7 = 4 \times 4$$
$$1 + 3 + 5 + 7 + 9 = 5 \times 5$$

When the pattern is analysed it becomes possible to *predict* the sum of the first 10 odd numbers, or the first 1000 odd numbers, without having to calculate. Asking *why* this relationship exists invites children into the fascinating world of numbers where there are always logical explanations to be found and often intriguing facts to be explored along the way.

CHAPTER 2

Counting and Coming to Know Numbers

Before they start school, children have a rich experience of numbers that relate to their personal lives. Some are beginning to acquire diverse understandings that will be the basis for number sense. Initially the number facts that they know will be isolated, just as new words are learned singly before they are integrated into more flowing speech. The number four, for example, can be very significant when a child's own fourth birthday is anticipated. Many children will recognize the symbol for four, associating it with the '4' they have seen on a birthday card. Understanding the relationships that exist among numbers can, however, be complex as illustrated when the child tries to understand 'now you are three and soon you will be four', as the reasons for changing age do not appear to relate to any precise physical happening.

In these early stages, some differences between numbers can also be personally significant. For example, the ages of older friends and younger siblings may be used by parents to explain a variety of phenomena, from bedtimes, to allowances made for behaviour. These isolated uses of number words need to be reconciled with the logical system for counting that exists, and a variety of experiences are needed if young children are to master the sub-skills necessary to understand the ways numbers work. Experiences with objects and images will initially appear to be unrelated to the number words and symbols that they meet but connections will become more apparent through consistent use of numbers in meaningful activities.

Cardinal and ordinal aspects of number

There are two distinct ways in which numbers relate to sets of objects and these are referred to as the **cardinal** and the **ordinal** aspects of a number. A number is used in one sense to denote the size of a set and children will gradually come to recognize the

17

common characteristic in *four* candles, *four* wheels and *four* sweets, for example. Where objects in one set can be placed alongside objects in another, the practical experiences of matching will help children to identify one meaning of the number word '*four*' as the quantity in each of the sets. This identification of a number word with the quantity in a set is referred to as the **cardinal** (or **quantity**) aspect of number. It involves skills in matching and pattern recognition as children use the number words *two*, *three* and *four* before they identify them within the structure of the counting system. The tactile experiences of moving objects around and perhaps lining them up alongside each other will reinforce the sameness in quantity in a way that is not possible if static images alone are used. Where the context gives a meaning for this matching activity, children will understand the purpose more readily than abstract tasks that are found on worksheets in a classroom. For example, *three* bears, *three* bowls, *three* spoons, *three* chairs and *three* beds in the story of Goldilocks all help children understand the meaning of three.

A different use of number words occurs when they locate a position in the counting sequence. For example, a child might count steps on the way to bed: 'one, two, three, four . . .' In this case the word *four* is uttered after *three* and before *five*, and refers to the *fourth* step from the beginning rather than the collection of the first four steps together. The identification of a number with its position in a sequence is referred to as the **ordinal** (or **location**) aspect of number. In order to count in this way it is necessary not only to know the correct sequence of number words but also to co-ordinate this in a one-to-one correspondence with the objects being counted, memorizing those that have already been counted and those that remain.

Importance of counting for explaining numbers

To appreciate the connection between a sequence of number words and a collection of objects requires a combination of verbal, visual and tactile experiences that all give cognitive cues about the process of counting. Nunes and Bryant describe counting as 'a system which is partly an expression of universal laws and partly a bundle of convenient but arbitrary conventions' (Nunes and Bryant, 1996, p. 22). In order to identify some of the complexities that arise, they note that naming the numbers has a 'place-value' structure which does not become clear until the larger number names are reached. The name for 'fifty-three' probably makes more sense as 'five tens and three units' than 'eleven' which is difficult to identify as 'one ten and one unit'. In their early experiences children have to memorize a large collection of names and images. Only later will these be pieced together to reveal the underlying logical structure.

Much like early language learning, counting develops through a process in which the child can often take the initiative and a little encouragement will help to establish some of the basic knowledge upon which counting is built. Penny Munn (1997) talks of 'multiple overlapping developments in verbal, motor and cognitive activities that become integrated with each other over time'. She proposes that children's *beliefs* about counting are central to their development and discusses intervention activities that can lead young children into counting. Such activities involve:

- taking young children's counting seriously even when it is purely verbal and does not appear to have a purpose;
- stimulating children to develop their own numerical goals and use counting in relation to their personal lives;
- making the purpose of counting explicit to children;
- assessing children's beliefs about counting before comparing sets or working on adding and subtracting.

notes that 'it is not until children acquire some experience of mental activities involved in other people's counting' that they are able to 'internalise the cultural practice of counting' (Munn, 7, p. 18).

Learning to count

here are many skills to be acquired on the way to mastering counting and a rich network of connections is needed that cannot be *given* to children but must be learned through experiences in the real world and then expressed in the formal language and symbols of mathematics. Because counting is a powerful unifying idea in early number work, several research studies have analysed

19

the stages of learning and the skills that are integrated in being able to count 'properly'. From pre-counting experiences with words that relate to quantities through to the co-ordination of hand, eye, memory and cognitive schema for recording numerical data, there is the potential for confusion if support is not available for children to 'test out' their developing ideas about numbers. The involvement of an interested adult or an older child who is willing to engage in discussions about numbers will give a head start to those learning to count.

Pre-counting experiences

Very young children will develop an understanding of *pre-number* ideas, for example the word 'more' is often used with confidence when quantities are increased. It has been shown that young children of 2 and 3 years exhibit number sense where they are able to distinguish sets of two or three items although they may not yet know the number words to describe such sets (Gelman and Gallistel, 1978). When children were shown a plate with three mice and the same plate with one mouse surreptitiously removed, they looked around and under the plate showing that they knew one was missing even though they did not have words to describe what had happened. At this stage the number names have little meaning and it will be some time before isolated number words are associated with an ordering of quantities. By asking 3- and 4-year-olds if they would prefer *five* sweets or *three* sweets (or other such pairs of numbers), the same researchers assessed children's understanding of the number words and found that they were unable to compare two sets by the number words alone.

Meaningful contexts

Children can, however, begin to operate logically with numbers from an early age, and Martin Hughes (1986) showed how they can display sound understanding of numerical relationships when there is a meaningful context. He documented children's difficulties working with abstract questions and showed that the same problems could be solved when set in real situations. In one task, three cubes were placed in a tin and shown to the children. When one was then taken out, without seeing inside the tin, even 3-year-olds knew that there were two cubes left. However, they became confused when asked the question 'What is three take away two?' Hughes compared children's responses to real and abstract tasks and concluded that it is not always their number sense that is being tested. Where children were given a situation that they could think about in order to give meaning to a numerical question they were able to make sense of the question. Even where the situation was an imagined one, their success rates were higher than for purely abstract problems. This has implications for the classroom, as the move from real experiences to abstract thinking can present great difficulties for some children. Children need to progress from practical experiences to working with imagery of those experiences and they will also need to identify for themselves appropriate images for tackling different problems. Later chapters will discuss the way in which calculation strategies can be developed using different visual imagery.

Stages and progression

Counting is a complex process involving many sub-skills and it takes children a considerable time to become competent. Learning to count takes place in a social environment so that parents and carers are the first 'teachers', introducing ideas involving numbers. They will not plan a progressive programme but may, quite naturally, involve children in reciting the counting sequence through games, rhymes and stories. This is an important part of a child's experience as reciting number sequences is a basic skill needed for counting. Memorizing rhymes and songs can provide a child's first experiences of counting forwards and backwards; and using many different rhymes will help to establish consistency in ordering number words.

At the same time there are other skills that researchers have associated with 'stages' in the development of number and Schaeffer *et al.* (1974) characterize three stages that mark children's developing understanding of number:

- '*Stage One*' children can understand the meaning of 'more' (but not 'less'), can discriminate between small numbers on the basis of their perceptual patterns and can distinguish between larger and smaller collections provided they are lined up to show a 1–1 correspondence.

- '*Stage Two*' children can determine numbers from one to four by recognition or counting but for larger numbers their counting becomes inaccurate with difficulties co-ordinating speech with counting. They may understand the cardinal aspect for very small collections but have not yet related the two aspects for numbers greater than four.
- '*Stage Three*' children can count up to ten reasonably accurately and are beginning to connect the count for any set (the ordinal aspect) with the number that represents the whole collection (the cardinal aspect). They can use a count to find the size of a collection but cannot compare collections by their number name only.

Dickson *et al.* (1984) discussed these stages in detail in their review of such research and concluded that 'the child has to construct for himself the connection between the recitation of arbitrary sounds and the size of a collection'.

Small number pattern recognition

Through everyday activities, children can gain experience of sorting and comparing collections of objects and some will appreciate certain patterns that help to distinguish one set from another. Particularly notable are those associations that can be made with the children themselves. For example, 'two' can be identified with one in each hand and an extra one may lead to the notion of 'three'. The spatial arrangements for one, two and three are recognized earliest, then four objects arranged in a square – and one in the centre makes five, just like the dots on a dice. It is common for children to recognize five as it appears on a dice, but not when objects are arranged as a row of three together with a row of two. This is an example of a situation where the rearrangement of objects will help children to understand that the same number word applies so long as no more objects are added and none are taken away. Later, the representation of five as a set of fingers on one hand (and ten as two hands) will be important for supporting calculating strategies. Talking about these arrangements with friends or an adult will help children to develop strategies for rearranging and recognizing quantities and for using early number language. However, without appropriate interactions, the activities can remain meaningless. When patterns or special arrangements of objects are instantly recognized, this skill is called *subitizing*. There is no counting involved but a spatial arrangement becomes familiar and it is consistently associated with the same number word.

Matching in a one-to-one correspondence

Sets can be compared by making a *one-to-one correspondence* between the objects in the sets to see which has the greater number (Figure 2.1a). The activity of lining up objects in rows or towers to make a comparison involves checking that both have the same 'starting point' from which the quantities will be viewed. Notions of more and fewer/less will be identified with which line is longest or which tower is tallest. At the same time, children may be misled by physical characteristics like the image presented when a row of small objects appears shorter than a longer row of large objects although the number in each row may be the same. Children will believe that the spatial arrangement of a collection can affect the quantity and that a collection has more in it when it is spread out (Figure 2.1b).

Piaget (1965) identified '*conservation*' as the concept that enables children to realize that quantity is not affected by any re-arrangement and he demonstrated that young children are frequently misled by their intuitive judgements. In his classic experiments, when two rows of objects were *matched*, young children appreciated that there was the same quantity in each but when one of the row was spread out or brought together they thought the rows no longer had the same quantity of items.

Many researchers have replicated Piaget's tests and show that in the early stages even children who can count do not make their judgement by counting but use perceptual judgements and may easily be misled. Fuson (1988) designed some experiments that attempted to lead children to use other than perceptual strategies by colour matching the objects in two sets and first comparing sets where there were no misleading cues, for example. She showed that

23

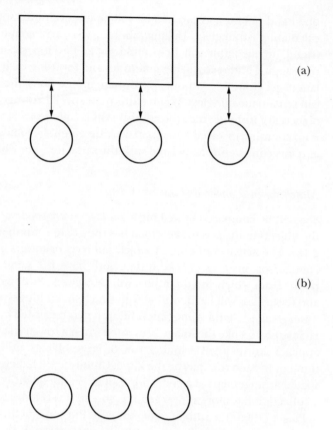

Figure 2.1 (a) Matching in a *one-to-one correspondence*.
(b) A row of small objects may appear to be less than a longer
row of large objects.

4- and 5-year-olds still relied on misleading length cues when
comparing the sizes of two sets even when they could obtain
information by counting.

The cardinality principle – naming a collection

In a progression in the skills that children acquire on the way to
effective counting, the early skill of *pattern recognition* (which is
developed in children as young as 2 years old) is followed much

later by the skill to give a number name to a collection. When children start counting collections of objects they point to items ⌐e at a time and are most likely to be unaware that the single ⌐umber word that ends the count represents the totality of the collection. This recognition and ability to name the whole set is called the *cardinality principle*. The words that are used to identify different sub-skills are not important, but the knowledge that there is a step in transferring from counting in ones to this use of numbers to designate a whole collection may explain why some children appear to be slow in progressing with their number work. To combine '3' and '2' in any form of addition will be difficult if the 3 is associated only with an individual object (the one that is pointed at as the word 'three' is uttered) and not with the whole collection of three objects.

A '*skill integrationist*' perspective on the way children learn was proposed by Schaeffer *et al.* (1974) as they suggested how the ability to count effectively develops over a period of time. By recognizing the spatial arrangement for naming a collection of two or three objects, and identifying this with the verbal count for a one-to-one correspondence, children are able to deduce that the last counting word is the name given to the collection. With the ability to recognize a pattern for four or five objects, an association with the longer counting sequence is made and so the mental connection is made between the 'name' for the last object and the 'name' for the whole set. By making logical deductions and testing their own thinking, children will begin to experience the underlying structures that unify counting and number patterns. It is at this stage that number sense begins to develop as they come to understand the different roles that numbers and number words can play.

Other researchers have identified a transition that is evident when the ordinal and the cardinal aspects of numbers come to be related in children's thinking. Steffe *et al.* (1983) referred to a transfer that is made from the *component* nature of numbers to their *composite* nature. Pupils also need to progress from understanding a 'unit' as a single object (a singleton unit) and a 'unit' as a group of objects (a composite unit) (SCAA, 1997, p. 5). Understanding that 'ten' can be both ten individual items and at the same time a 'ten' that is counted as 'one ten' is necessary for understanding place value. Until this distinction is understood, progress in calculating cannot be made. Making these links between the different uses of numbers and counting will give children powerful mental strategies for problem solving and these will be explored further in later chapters.

Abstraction principle – what can be counted

In identifying the procedures that need to be mastered in early counting, Gelman and Gallistel (1978) proposed the *abstraction principle* that deals with the definition of what is countable. The range of entities that children perceive to be countable increases with experience but is often not as limited as school schemes may indicate (many things can be counted – seen or unseen, sounds, movements, 'pairs!', hundreds and quarters). What children can count is often related to their personal pre-school experiences. For example, Ellie (four years, two months), who lives opposite a church with a clock that chimes the hour, has learned to count the chimes because she understands the relevance certain times have for her daily routine. In their research Gelman and Gallistel found that pre-school children could count diverse and heterogeneous sets (for example, assorted trinkets and shells) and their accuracy seemed to be unaffected by the introduction of diverse materials. They concluded that 'young children can readily group a variety of two-dimensional and three-dimensional materials under the rubric of "things to be counted." '

The idea of what children can count was developed further by Steffe *et al.* (1983) who identified five different types of countable item of progressive difficulty:

- *perceptual* units: items that can be identified as discrete 'things' to be counted as children would count a collection of buttons;
- *figural* units: items that are not immediately available but are recalled and imagined (for example, the pets a child has at home);
- *motor* units: items that are motor acts like pointing, or movements like steps;
- *verbal* units: utterances like number words that can themselves be counted (for example, saying '8, 9, 10' and knowing three numbers had been counted);

- *abstract* units: items that can be introduced by the child to 'match' the count for any given number.

This progression takes children from seeing, touching and counting 'actual' objects to understanding that the abstract number itself may be identified with the count that generates it (for example 'eight' by itself implies the sequence 'one, two, ... eight'). School experiences are too often limited to static collections on workcards and some children fail to develop to the level of abstraction that is necessary to operate effectively with numbers.

Order-irrelevance principle

The *order-irrelevance principle* 'captures the way' different skills 'interact in contributing to a full appreciation of what counting is about' (Gelman and Gallistel, 1978, p. 141). Number tags can be given to any of the objects as long as there is one for each and all objects are included. It does not matter which number tag is assigned to which item and the count can 'jump around' to attach the numbers in order to the items. This principle is demonstrated when moving objects, for example fish in a tank, or children in a playground, are to be counted and it may take several attempts to complete the task with different starting points and different strategies for keeping track.

Summarizing the stages

By understanding the stages in learning to count and the range of skills to be mastered, teachers can monitor progress and provide activities that will address particular sub-skills that are not yet well established. The stages of learning to count have been summarized by Thompson (1997) as follows:

- *recitation*: being able to recite the number words in their correct sequence;
- *enumeration*: assigning the correctly ordered number words in one-to-one correspondence with the objects being counted;
- *cardinality*: realizing that the number assigned to the final object counted tells how many there are in the whole collection.

Thompson goes on to identify activities that will help children to develop the individual skills and notes that 'only when children can successfully satisfy all three . . . criteria can it be said they are able to count' (Thompson, 1997, p. 131).

In supporting the view that there are many diverse skills that children will only master over an extended period of time, Nunes and Bryant (1996) refer to a variety of researchers' experiments where the results suggest that children initially learn to count without understanding that counting is a measure of set size. They conclude that 'it is one thing to be able to count and answer the question "how many?" but quite another to understand the significance of the number uttered at the end of counting as a measure of set size' (Nunes and Bryant, 1996, p. 41).

Developing counting skills

When children start school, many are skilled counters (some in a more limited sense than others) but they traditionally spend some time in school with 'pre-number' activities like matching, ordering and colouring which they cannot easily relate to their existing knowledge. Although such skills need to be developed in children's school experiences, their use may be better related to classifying shapes in mathematics or to science activities where the consequent outcomes can be associated with establishing the relevant characteristics of, for example, objects, fruits or animals. It is questionable whether the associated activities are adding to the children's number understanding and they can serve to detach school work from the useful purposes of numbers (Whitebread, 1999, p. 28). Thompson (1997) questions whether there is a transfer of learning from such activities to situations involving numbers. His book, *Teaching and Learning Early Number,* is based on the principle that counting should be the fundamental mathematical process that needs to be addressed from the child's earliest experiences in school.

As well as learning to recognize some small number patterns, children in school can start by reciting number words as a social activity that reinforces the universal nature of counting. Together they can begin to enjoy the stability of the counting sequence, acquiring rhythm and pace as they develop a feeling for verbal patterns. This play with words should be encouraged as similar patterns and rhythms underpin many mathematical strategies in later problem solving. Such apparently simple rhymes as 'One, two, three. Mother caught a flea ...', for example, have a rhythm that may be developed to 'one, two, *three*, four, five, *six*, ...' as a prerequisite pattern for learning the facts for multiplication by three (Anghileri, 1997, p. 47).

Introducing resources to develop mental imagery

In addition to developing verbal skills in counting, children will use visual imagery to help them establish the patterns and relationships that exist within the counting sequence. A 'bead frame' or 'bead string' of ten beads made up of sets of five beads in two different colours serves as an introduction to the numbered line that is one of the most useful images for relating numbers and counting. Counting along the line of beads will provide further visual images of numbers that reflect the relationships that exist, for example that six is one more than five. Each child can have a personal 'bead string' of ten beads to organize and re-organize. As well as relating the images to the counting sequence, the arrangements generated by 'splitting' the beads into two sets will illustrate all the number pairs that make ten. The ideas and images relate well to the ten fingers that are arranged on two hands, which also provide an invaluable resource for developing imagery for the number relationships that can be found in a set of ten.

Number bonds in ten

The number pairs that together combine to make ten can be memorized to provide important 'benchmarks' as known facts from which other combinations can be derived. There are many games and puzzles available that are based on the pairs of numbers that together make ten. Initially some form of images will be important for checking and children can be encouraged to talk about the numbers that relate in this way. Some puzzles have a self-checking element involving co-ordinated colours or interlocking pieces so that children can play on their own. The intention is to give children instant recall of numbers that together make ten and also to develop their understanding of the links that exist between the numbers. From '5 and 5 make 10', for example, they can be encouraged to shift one across to make '4 and 6' so that the facts are not isolated. Although some children learn the relationships for themselves when they realize their significance, visual images will be helpful and all children will benefit from teacher interventions to highlight these important connections.

Working beyond ten

Later, children need images that can be associated with the counting sequence beyond ten. These can be provided with a 100 square where the numbers are arranged to show the place value structure of the numbers, or a bead string of 100 beads in two colours arranged in tens. Moving across rows and columns of the 100 square can be associated with counting. Counting forwards and counting backwards can also be associated with movement along the number line. Initially, movements one at a time can be associated with 'hops'; later, 'jumps' can be associated with larger intervals (Menne, 2000). These actions can be associated with addition and subtraction as children are encouraged to recognize the movements that are needed to get from one number to another. There is a progressive development:

- working 'within ten' (focusing on number facts with totals up to ten);
- counting 'across to ten', recognizing jumps to the nearest ten;
- jumps of ten at a time.

Figure 2.2 A 'tens catcher'.

The illustration (Figure 2.2) shows a 'tens catcher' that has been developed to give images on the bead string of what happens when ten is added to or subtracted from any number (Menne, 2000).

Research has shown that images starting with the bead string can be modified progressively to a number line, and then an 'empty number line' (that is a line with no marking at all) to provide mental imagery for calculating strategies based on counting (Beishuizen, 1999). The 'empty number line' introduces the flexibility to take 'jumps' of any size in either direction and mental strategies associated with this imagery will be discussed more fully in the following chapters.

Developing flexibility in counting

The unitary counting sequence, counting in ones, starts as a list of numbers that can be recited in a particular order and once children are confident to start at one they can be encouraged to start at any number. Counting that starts, for example, at the number seven is more demanding than starting at one as it is rather like trying to complete the lines of a song or poem but starting in the middle. When children meet addition this will be an essential skill as 'counting-on' is one of the effective strategies in the early stages. Even where the counting sequence can be recited, 'double counting' will be needed to keep track when 'counting-on' is used. To calculate 8 + 3, for example, by saying 'eight, *nine, ten, eleven*' requires the words '*nine, ten, eleven*' to be matched with a count of three. Using fingers, tapping or some other physical movement may be helpful to keep track of the three number words used to count beyond eight.

Subtraction can involve counting backwards and this needs to be practised by asking for a particular number of steps, which will also require children to maintain two counts at the same time. To calculate 8 − 3 involves starting at eight and counting back three 'steps': '8 − 7, 6, 5'. This time one of the counts is backwards (7, 6, 5) while the other is a mental count forwards (1, 2, 3) to keep track. Again, fingers can be used to help keep track or a number line can be used to model the steps (Figure 2.3).

Figure 2.3 Calculating 8 − 3 on a number line.

When multiplication is linked to counting, a triple count is necessary. Two counts relate to the individual items: one count matches a counting word with each item, while a second count monitors the fact that every set has the same number of elements.

'1, 2, 3, . . . 4, 5, 6, . . . 7, 8, 9, . . . '
1, 2, 3   1, 2, 3   1, 2, 3
1   2   3

A third count is necessary to 'tally' the number of sets that have been accounted for (Anghileri, 1995, 1997, p. 46).

Extending counting patterns

As well as counting in ones, children can enjoy other number patterns such as counting in twos, threes, fives and tens. Although these different counts will initially be lists of numbers with little meaning, the way in which they are constructed will familiarize children with the systematic patterns that underlie some important mathematical structures such as the multiplication facts. There will be opportunities for *generalizing* the rules as they extend for themselves a count such as '5, 10, 15, 20, 25 . . .', identifying which number comes next. This can introduce the challenge of extending the patterns beyond 100, which will use and help to reinforce understanding of the way numbers are constructed.

By learning the patterns for different numbers, children can become familiar with the 'nice' numbers, such as 12 or 36, that appear frequently and the 'not so nice' numbers, such as 13 or 23, which rarely appear. The reader will recognize that 13 and 23 are prime numbers that have no factors (other than themselves and one) but such definitions will only appear later in school. The benefit of working with number patterns and different counting sequences is that children develop a 'feel' for numbers that will have positive benefits in helping their later calculating skills.

CHAPTER 3

Towards a System of Symbols

In the same way that children's early writing does not reflect their ability with words, recorded work with numbers cannot represent the mathematical thinking that they have mastered. The practice children get in forming symbols will not add to their understanding initially but will give them the conventions they need for communicating ideas in writing. For this reason it is important that they continue to develop mental strategies and that much of their mathematical thinking throughout primary school takes place through oral work. The stimulus for working with numbers can be a real problem, or a practical activity, and children enjoy any ideas that relate to their personal lives. Alternatively, the starting point can be puzzles and games that help them to recognize the symbols and begin to appreciate the ordering and relationships that are important.

Activities that generate written recording need to make purposeful use of children's own recording, for example where 'cards' are made by the children themselves for matching or memory games. Price labels for a classroom shop or lists of prices for a café can be made and then sorted and re-sorted for use in many types of display. In practising to read and write numerals, children can be involved in activities that reflect the usefulness of numbers. This will motivate them to ask questions and talk about relationships.

Symbols for numbers

In learning the symbols to represent numbers, associations are made with many different situations in which these numbers are used, but children will also need to understand the more abstract nature of a number. Gray and Tall (1994) introduce the term '*procept*' to try and explain the ambiguity that exists between the symbols that are introduced to represent mathematical *concepts* and the *processes* involved in developing these concepts. Understanding

33

Figure 3.1 Different images of 'six'.

'six' includes the various ways six may be decomposed and recom-
posed, and many of these ideas will be evident in pictorial
representation of six objects where the pattern can be seen in
different ways. Gray and Tall suggest that the procept 'six' includes
the process of counting six and at the same time a growing collection of other representations such as 'three and three', 'three lots
of two', 'one more than five' and so on (Figure 3.1).

The more varied the patterns that children can readily associate
with the symbol 6, the better will be their preparation for incorpo-
rating these ideas into problem-solving strategies. Gray and Tall
believe that 'ambiguity in interpreting symbolism in this flexible
way is at the root of successful mathematical thinking' and they
'regard a symbol as something that is perceived by the senses. It can
be written or spoken so that it can be seen or heard'. What is
interesting is the way symbols are interpreted differently by individuals or by the same individual at different times. Some children

appear confused because they are unsure of the convention that applies in a particular situation. Reading 23, for example, as 'twenty-three' rather than 'two, three' is a convention in the same way that reading 2.30 as 'two thirty' is a convention associated with time.

In later number work, the ideas needed for 'reading' decimal numbers may cause confusion for some children, as understanding will often involve the relationships that are implicit in the number system. The decimal '0.25' is read as 'nought point two five' but it represents 25 hundredths and half of 0.5. These associations are more useful than knowing the 0.25 is '2 tenths and 5 hundredths' although this would be the extension of place value ideas to numbers less than one. Some children are not helped as their familiarity with such decimals for symbolizing money and the use of £1.25 to represent 'one pound and twenty-five pence' leaves them with a notion that 5 represents the 'units' in this sum. The inclusion of zero, as in 1.04, is also a source of confusion and some children find this number difficult to distinguish from 1.4.

The nature and levels of development of a procept are dependent on the cognitive growth and experiences of the child. Just as the number 3 may at first be associated with birthdays and candles, as the child acquires more experiences it is associated with 'the number before 4' and 'half of 6'. Sometimes, the words used give no clues to their representation, for example, ten, eleven, twelve and so on. Children will take time to understand the way larger numbers are constructed using a place value system with the ten basic symbols 0, 1, 2, 3, 4, 5, 6, 7, 8 and 9. This is a sophisticated system as millions of different numbers can be constructed from the same symbols placed in different positions, e.g. '3.2' is different from '32'.

Children have to learn to 'read' numbers like 32 and to understand what they can mean, just as they have to learn to read and interpret words in different ways in their language learning, depending on the context. Fuson *et al.* (1997) describe 'three correct conceptions' of numbers used by children:

- *unitary conception* related to counting in ones up to 32;
- *sequencing conception* related to counting by tens and then by ones – 10, 20, 30, 31, 32;
- *separate tens and ones* – 1 ten, 2 tens, 3 tens and 1 unit, 2 units.

Images associated with *sequence* conception include the number line or 'jumps on the empty number line' (Beishuizen, 1999; Menne, 2000). *Separate tens and ones* are more readily associates with structured materials such as sticks of ten multilink cubes and separate cubes, or Dienes-type 'tens rods' and 'unit cubes'. Difficulty in understanding the need for distinction between these two interpretations becomes clearer when the assessment question 'How many tens in 43?' is incorrectly answered '40'. Such a response would suggest that pupils have some understanding of the idea of tens but have not yet made the transition from 'unit' as 'one' and 'unit' as 'group' (in this case a 'ten') (SCAA, 1997, p. 5). Fuson *et al.* (1997) describe another view of numbers as a '*concatenated single-digit conception*' in which the number is thought of as two separate digits, 'three two', and associate this notion with premature introduction of column arithmetic involving 'tens and units'. Advice from the Schools Curriculum and Assessment Authority (SCAA) in the UK talks about the importance of the idea of a 'unit' and the way a collection of ten units itself becomes a 'unit ten' for calculating and for recording.

Research in the UK has shown that, even at secondary school, many pupils still have difficulties with understanding place value (Brown, 1981a). One of the questions involved a meter that counts the people going into a football stand and shows:

Pupils were asked to show the meter after *one* more person has gone in:

This was answered correctly by 68% of 12-year-olds (88% of 15-year-olds). A correct response depends on understanding the way numbers are constructed and shows that working with such large numbers continues to be challenging for older children.

Language difficulties

Language is central in learning about numbers and understanding at all stages will be influenced by the words that are used in discussions, questioning and explanations. Although many children readily relate their growing understanding of numbers to symbolic representation, the formalization of words and symbols may present difficulties where ambiguities are not explored. Some research analysing learning difficulties has taken as a major focus the irregularities in English words for two-digit numbers (Fuson *et al.*, 1997). Patterns are most easily seen in the larger numbers, for example, six thousand eight hundred, but the teens (thirteen, fourteen, fifteen) and early decade numbers (ten, twenty, thirty) do not conform to the regular pattern of 'number of tens' and 'number of units' (for example, sixty-four: six tens and four units). The words 'eleven' and 'twelve' bear little relationship to the 'one ten and one' and 'one ten and two' that are used to symbolize them. Even where the words are regular, confusion may arise from the abbreviated format of the symbols and a common error is for children to record 'thirty-two' literally as 302. Resources such as 'arrow cards' can be introduced to show how numbers are constructed (Figure 3.2)

The number words themselves and the symbols we use provide a shorthand representation in which numerical relationships are implicit. Traditional teaching in many countries has emphasized the place value aspect of notation, splitting numbers into 'tens' and 'units'. The emphasis on being able to say that there are '6' tens in 62 may be helpful in speedy written vertical calculations and the emphasis on teaching standard algorithms has justified this approach in the past. In schools today, vertical recording is not the central way of recording calculations. If such methods are introduced before pupils can carry out calculations mentally, this can hinder the development of mental strategies and lead to misunderstandings and mistakes (Fuson, 1992, p. 243).

Research suggests that undue emphasis on the place value structure may invite a *digitwise* approach to calculating which will generate many errors. Instead of concentrating only on partitioning numbers into their constituent 'tens' and 'ones', understanding the structure of whole numbers may be helped by

37

Figure 3.2 Arrow cards to show how numbers are constructed.

partitioning numbers in a variety of ways. 'For example, being taught to treat 62 as 60 and 2, or 50 and 12, or 70 less 8', according to the different contexts in which the number is used, 'may provide a better understanding of number structure and help pupils develop effective mental strategies' (SCAA, 1997, p. 8). This approach is sometimes identified as a *holistic* approach in which numbers are kept as wholes in any partition. Once again, the use of real examples will help illustrate the importance of different partitions: 60 seconds and 2 more; 50 pence and 12 more; 8 cm short of 70 cm.

To develop number sense, it is important to introduce 'chunking' in a variety of ways. As well as being 30 and 6, 36 is 32 + 4 or 20 + 16, and different 'chunks' may be associated with addition and subtraction, or with multiplication and division. The choice of partition can be crucial in finding the most efficient way to perform a calculation, as an example for calculating 1256 ÷ 6 shows (Figure 3.3).

For larger numbers such as 1256, it becomes important for children to recognize that place values may be expressed differently

1256 apples are divided among 6 shopkeepers.
How many apples will every shopkeeper get?
How many apples will be left?

Working: $100 \times 6 = 600$ Answer: 136....

$1000 \div 6 = 106 r 2$

$200 \div 6 = \cancel{480 r} \cancel{18r20}\ 198\ 2/r2$

$50 \div 6 = 8 r 2$

$6 \div 6 = 1$

$106 + 21 + 8 + 1 = 136$

$2 + 2 + 2 = 6$

Figure 3.3 Calculating $1256 \div 6$.

as 125 tens or 12 hundreds and 56. Seeing that 1256 is not only
1000+200+50+6 but also 1200+56 would have made the calculation so much easier.

Looking for patterns

By working with written symbols, the logical structure of numbers
can become more apparent, as patterns in the way numbers are
'built' may be related to visual imagery based on different classroom resources. The process of adding ten to any number, for
example, can be illustrated on a 100 square by 'moving down' a row.
Alternatively, working with 10p and 1p coins can show how a 10p
coin added to 32p (three 10p and 2p) will result in 42p (four 10p

39

and 2p). As an explicit illustration of the ways in which numbers are built, Gattegno charts can be used to practise naming and representing numbers with whole classes. Faux (1998) describes routines such as pointing to 800 on the chart as the children chant 'eight hundred' and then 50 as they say 'fifty' and then 3 as they say 'three'. In this way the words 'eight hundred and fifty-three' come to be associated with 800 and 50 and 3 as well as with 853.

Another practical teaching approach has been to 'model' the number system using cubes and rods. Such models emphasize the 'unit' ten structure with sticks of 'tens' that can be handled as a single unit. These are designed to encourage 'four' as the accepted answer to 'How many tens in 45?' but children's ability to transfer from understanding the models to seeing how these 'represent' the structure and the way to manipulate numbers is questionable. Hart (1989) concluded that the manipulation of blocks to illustrate the algorithm for subtraction was not effective as 'the gap between the two types of experience is too large' and pupils saw little connection. 'The phenomenon is that children may show the ability to subtract numbers higher than ten when dealing with blocks or coins but seem to lose it in the transfer to symbolic notation.'

Building connections between the variety of visual imagery that is available and the abstract relationships that exist among numbers will also help children to develop the strategies they will need for calculating. In addition to jumps of ten on a number line, working with missing numbers in a hundred square can be related to adding and subtracting tens and multiples of ten (Figure 3.4).

This idea can then be related to jumps of eleven or nine on the number line, and adding a 'tens stick' as connections are made between the numbers and between the different images.

Symbols for operations

As well as symbols for numbers, children have to learn to use curtailed recording that involves symbols for operations and for processes in calculating. In the early years, recording will relate to results that the children have found out by their active involvement in practical tasks, or will help in identifying patterns with numbers.

?	27	?
36	37	38
?	?	48

Figure 3.4 Missing numbers on a 100 square.

Progression in learning to do calculations may be summarized as:

DOING ... TALKING ABOUT ... WRITING ABOUT ... SYMBOLIZING

Written recording will begin with pictorial representations that closely relate to the images presented by materials, and gradually the images will be replaced by appropriate mathematical symbols.

Over-simplification in the use and interpretation of symbols like the operation signs, '+, −, ×, ÷', or the equals sign, '=', may appear to be effective in the short term since replacing words with symbols requires less well developed manipulative skills, but on the other hand will certainly lead to limited interpretation and may lead to later confusion. The subtraction symbol '−', for example, has many interpretations including 'take away', 'subtract', 'minus', 'difference between', and may be used to represent problems of 'fewer than' or 'less than'.

Traditionally the symbols for addition and subtraction have been introduced early in a child's school experience and the teacher's role has been to explain their meaning and to instruct children in procedures for carrying out calculations. Although most children have readily adapted to the 'codes' implicit in these symbolic

41

manipulations, the need to offer simple explanations in the early stages has led to difficulties when more complex meanings have been associated with the symbols. As an example, the idea of 'take away' as the interpretation for the subtraction symbol has led to uncertainty about 'difference' problems where comparison, rather than removal of object, is required (for example, Tom is 6 years old and Amy is 8. What is the difference in their ages?). Current recommendations propose that 'oral and mental competence' is established 'before written calculation methods are introduced' (DfEE, 1998, p. 51). This does not mean that there will be no written recording but that children will learn to record their thinking with progressive formalization, learning first to use words to record results they can already talk about. This should include discussions about the way they themselves and their peers could record their findings with symbols introduced as a shorthand for the words they are using.

In addition to the traditional format of sums, the symbols for addition and subtraction can be used in flexible ways. Arrows are useful as they do not require the 'equals' symbols which can add complications in interpreting written statements such as $5 = 3 + 2$

$$(3 \text{ and } 2) \xrightarrow{\text{together make}} 5$$

The symbolic statement $3 + 2$ represents both the process of adding, whether through the image of physical objects or a counting pattern. The concept of the sum that is the answer to the calculation and is another example of the procepts identified by Gray and Tall (1994). Understanding $3 + 2 = 5$ involves interpreting the symbols, understanding the concepts of 'add' and 'equals' and the processes associated with finding a solution.

Research has shown that more successful children use symbols both as objects to be manipulated and as triggers to evoke mathematical processes, with flexible ways to interpret the mathematical symbols and the numbers themselves (Anghileri, 1999b). Take the mental strategy of 'near doubles' identified in the Framework for Teaching Mathematics from Reception to Year 6 (1999) and the particular example $6 + 5$. This becomes an easy calculation, using the known fact that $5 + 5$ makes 10, only if 6 is associated readily with 5 and 1 more. An equally efficient approach could be to recall the number bonds of 10 where $6 + 4$ is a readily recalled total. Again, this can only be useful if 5 is associated with 4 and 1 more. This flexible use of symbols is developed alongside early recording where the pace allows discussion alongside the practising of manipulative skills.

A calculator can be a valuable additional aid to help children to relate number symbols to words and to practical applications involving all kinds of numbers. As well as motivating children to think about symbols, a calculator can provide a personal, self-correcting aid to learning about patterns and sequences of numbers. With a simple 'four-function' calculator, keying in '1', '+', '+' then repeatedly '='..., automatically generates the counting sequence that can be used to keep a tally of anything that is being counted. Similarly, '2', '+', '+' will get the calculator counting in twos. At a more advanced stage, ask the question, 'Will the calculator show 100 when it counts in threes?' and you have the type of investigation that can provoke thinking about the numbers that are multiples of three and why 100 is not there. Early use of more powerful graphics calculators can have the advantage of showing the whole calculation on the screen where other calculators show only the result of any calculation.

Developing a 'feel' for numbers

Where number experiences involve a variety of situations and contexts, children will begin to develop a 'feel' for numbers that will be the foundation for calculating strategies and for using numbers effectively for problem-solving. Consider, for example, the numbers 16 and 17. Although very close in size, 16 has a 'nice feel' about it being 'double 8' or '4 × 4', while 17 has fewer convenient relationships with other numbers. The 'double' numbers, which appear to be the easiest to remember as number bonds, all appear in the sequence of counting in twos. These numbers are also called '*even*' numbers while all the others which are not multiples of two are called '*odd*'. There is no easy way to remember these names although the visual image of an odd number of items can always involve an arrangement of pairs with one 'odd' item that cannot be paired. Since the mathematical meanings of these words, odd and even, are different from their meanings in ordinary English, some discussion will be necessary to establish the conventions that will be assumed when working with these numbers.

Figure 3.5 'Square', 'triangular' and 'cube' numbers.

Although the name '*even*' is given to all multiples of two, there are no particular names for multiples of three, four, five, etc. There are, however, characteristics that such numbers possess which can become familiar to children when the number symbols are used. Counting in fives gives only the numbers ending in 5 or 0, while counting in fours will give only even numbers. Counting in threes: '3, 6, 9, 12, 15, 18, 21, 24, 27, 30, . . .', will give numbers that are alternately odd and even and whose digits always add up to 3 or 6 or 9. Such 'discoveries' can be fascinating and attempts to explain the reasons behind these findings will help reinforce the logical nature of the number system and the patterns within it.

There will be some numbers that rarely appear in patterns

because they are not multiples of any other number. Numbers such as 13, 17 and 31 are multiples only of themselves and one, and are called '*prime*' numbers. What is fascinating about the prime numbers is the fact that they do not appear regularly in the counting sequence and there is no easy way to 'test' a number to see if it is prime, apart from trying all of the possible factors it could have. Other characterizations of numbers can include '*square*', '*triangular*' and '*cube*' numbers that are named because of the way they can be made with geometric arrangements (Figure 3.5).

Although numbers have a utilitarian nature for representing and solving problems, the number system has a beauty in the logical relationships that exist and the patterns that can be generated. Developing children's fascination for numbers will encourage not only 'number sense' but also an ability to observe and analyse relationships involving skills that will have applications throughout and beyond mathematics.

CHAPTER 4

Addition and Subtraction

The operations of addition and subtraction can be introduced through experiences relating to combining and partitioning collections of objects. Ideas of these operations begin to be formalized when the results are expressed using particular language, and later symbolic format. There are other operations on numbers that are not so readily formalized, for example halving and doubling, and it is important to remember that addition and subtraction form only part of a child's experiences with numbers. Rearranging collections can give a feel for numbers if there is discussion to accompany the activity, for example, 6 is 3 and 3, or 2 and 2 and 2, or 2 more than 4. In the early stages of learning about arithmetic operations, informal ideas are developed so that children are confident working orally and with diagrammatic representations before any symbols are introduced. With careful progression, the symbols will provide a shorthand way to record results that children already know, but premature introduction will cause difficulties.

The very words 'addition' and 'subtraction' make it clear that these arithmetic operations are a classroom formalization of certain processes that are associated with numbers. These words are rarely used outside school and many children will take time to associate them with their existing knowledge in the same way that it takes time to acquire new words and phrases in language. The terms themselves bring together a wealth of meanings that can be associated with the symbols '+' and '−'. Language such as 'add', 'plus', 'together make', 'take away', 'minus', 'subtract' and 'difference between' gives some indication of the diversity of language that needs to be mastered in children's developing understanding of context and situations that will later be symbolized.

Formalizing language

There are many stages in building links between new words, exist-ing experiences, and the knowledge of numbers that children already possess. In the first stages, children will begin to acquire informal understanding of addition and subtraction, both inside and outside the classroom, by observing patterns as they arrange and re-arrange collections. This will involve manipulation of real materials that children will later visualize, and it is important that children begin to talk about numbers so that they appreciate connections with their existing knowledge. In discussion children and teachers can talk about the way numbers relate to different situations and introduce words like 'altogether', 'makes', 'take away' and 'leaves', and expressions like 'one more, two more . . . ten more' and 'one less, two less . . . ten less'. In these early stages the focus should be on the number relationships that are generated, as much as the actions that are involved, since number sense develops as children become aware of the consistency in some of their findings.

They will come to know that '4 and 2 more' always results in 6, and that '4 and 3 more' is 7, one more than 6. Already there are connections to be made, as their 'bank' of known facts and strat-egies for deriving new facts is developed. Before any recording takes place the next stage involves refining the language for addi-tion and subtraction with expressions like '4 and 2 more' replaced by '4 add 2', and '4 take away 2' replaced by '4 subtract 2'. At this stage it is important to use a whole variety of language so that addition is about 'increasing' and 'more than', and subtraction includes 'difference between'. For example, two measures may be compared using a subtraction calculation: 'If a toy truck is balanced by eight cubes and a car is balanced by five cubes, what is the difference in their weights?' relates to 8 subtract 3.

Relating addition and subtraction to counting

The practical activity of adding one more to a collection, or taking one away will provide additional language and experiences with counting which will help children to associate the concrete models with some abstract number patterns. When the practical idea of 'one more' is associated with the next number in a counting sequence, and 'one less' is associated with the previous number, these patterns can begin to be identified with 'add one' and 'subtract one'. This is initially achieved through problems that have meaning for the children like adding beads to a necklace, sorting coloured counters for a game, or organizing the children themselves into groups. Many of the more contrived activities with classroom materials, like colouring pictures on a worksheet, leave the children confused about their purpose and provide little motivation for finding answers. When children are happy to respond verbally to questions about 'one more/add one' and 'one less/subtract one', representations including arrows, 'function machines' for changing numbers, and 'hops' on the number line may be introduced to record some findings (Figure 4.1). It is worth noting that none of the representations in Figure 4.1 involve the 'equals' symbol, which needs careful introduction if its true meaning is to be used and it is not restricted to the interpretation of 'makes'.

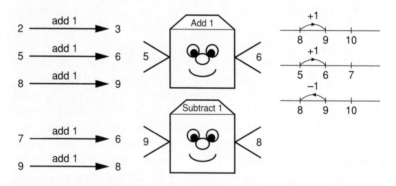

Figure 4.1 Recording 'one more' and 'one less' with 'arrows', 'function machines' and 'hops' on the number line.

Although it may be tempting to read the symbols '− 1' as 'take away one', this will limit the circumstances in which the symbol can be used and give a false impression of the meaning that will have to be re-learned later. The word 'minus' is also used but the association of 'add' with addition and 'subtract' with subtraction may be helpful. Numbers need not be limited in the activity of 'adding one'. As soon as children can count beyond twenty, larger numbers can be used to focus on the change that takes place as each 'decade number' is reached. For example, '16 add 1', '19 add 1' or '39 add 1' can be associated with addition and, at the same time, used to reinforce the vocabulary of counting. 'Subtract 1' may be similarly associated with counting backwards. Examples such as '20 subtract 1' can be used to assess children's understanding of the way the number system is constructed.

Practical problems

There is research evidence to show that very young pupils can find solutions to calculations even if they lack sophisticated mathematical techniques, suggesting that the mathematics is developed out of problem solving rather than learned separately and then applied (Carpenter and Fennema, 1989; Hughes, 1986; Beishuizen, 1995). Real activities like keeping the score in a bean bag catching game (or real questions like 'How many in the red team if one more comes in?') will motivate children to find answers to numerical problems. Dates on a calendar provide a familiar context for larger numbers (for example, 'Today is the 19th. What will be the date tomorrow?'). Games, songs and stories can also be used to breach the reality/abstraction divide and will introduce variety into situations that can involve numbers. For example, rhymes like 'Ten fat sausages sizzling in a pan' or 'Ten green bottles' can be acted out or modelled with finger actions.

Progressing to 'add 2'

The idea of 'add 2' is the next stage in this development and is associated with both the practical activity of adding two more objects to a set and also the more abstract notion of a number 'two further on' in the counting sequence. Practical activities of 'adding 2 more' can involve children in predicting the total, thereby helping establish the link with counting. Initially the count will be verbalized, but the children can then be encouraged to count in a whisper, and eventually 'count in your head'. Small numbers may relate to familiar number facts such as '4 and 2 more is 6' but larger numbers such as '20 and 2 more' or '29 and 2 more' will again help to establish relationships with the structure of the number system. This approach is different from the more usual introduction to addition where two small collections are put together and counted. It helps to establish the relationship between adding and counting and uses the idea that one of the numbers is used as the starting point for a counting procedure.

Progression in counting strategies for addition

In the more traditional introduction to addition, involving the combining of two sets of objects, there is progression evident in the procedures children use for finding the total number of objects. These procedures are identified by Carpenter and Moser (1983) in their analysis of children's addition and subtraction strategies. There are a number of stages that have been identified in procedures for finding the answer to '3 add 5'. In the first stage, a set of 3 objects (or fingers) is combined with a set of 5 objects (or fingers) and the sets are put together and all objects are counted '1, 2, 3 . . . 4, 5, 6, 7, 8̲' in a strategy termed '*counting all*'. At the next stage the inefficiency is recognized as children realize that it is not necessary to re-count the first set. The collection is now counted '3 . . . 4, 5, 6, 7, 8̲' in a procedure termed '*counting on*'. This counting is more complex than the first stage, since many young children are able to count more successfully when they start at one than when they start at any other number. It is also complicated by the need to maintain a double count ('4, 5, 6, 7, 8' identified with '1 more, 2 more, . . . 5 more') and some action may be needed so that physical movements support the count. It is at this stage that a misconception can occur when the first number uttered (the count for the first set) becomes confused with the numbers to be added. This can also be seen where children point to numbers on a number line and count the number symbols they touch instead of the spaces they move across. If this misconception is formed it may be necessary to encourage children to use materials and the 'count all' strategy as a check.

A further development in strategy occurs with the recognition that '3 add 5' gives the same total as '5 add 3' (this is known as the *commutative law for addition*) and Carpenter and Moser (1983) described this next stage as '*counting on from the larger*'. When this relationship is recognized, the count may be shortened to '5 . . . 6, 7, 8̲', sometimes supported by the imagined action of first 'putting the 5 in your head'. Children may be better motivated to use such a shortcut when larger numbers are introduced such as '2 add 15' and '3 add 49'. There is evidence that children progress through these stages of 'counting all', 'counting on' and 'counting on from the larger number' before they come to recognize that '3 and 5 together *always* make 8' – a *number fact*. It is by focusing on the number relationships that are generated, as well as the procedures for generating them, that children are helped in developing number sense.

Complications with addition may arise where the number zero is involved. The sum $5 + 0 = ?$ is often interpreted as '5 add nothing'. Therein lies an immediate difficulty – if there is nothing to add then what can the question be requiring? Teachers may give a context, for example, 'five cats are sitting on a wall and no more cats come along so how many cats are on the wall?' Too frequently this is seen by children as a ritualistic game with little purpose. Equally difficult can be subtractions like $5 - 5 = ?$ where the answer is zero. Problem like these, together with $5 - 0 = ?$ and later, $5 \times 0 = ?$, have important consequences when calculations with double digit numbers like 20 or 102 are involved. Teachers suggesting contexts may provide a short-term solution to the difficulty but, in general, it is only clear that children have understanding where they are able to provide their own context for such problems.

Observing children as they calculate will help identify the stage of development of each individual although this is not easy with a large class of children. Children who rely on counting the actual objects can be encouraged to visualize the situation by using a cover over the objects or working with their eyes shut to *think about* the objects involved. The next level of abstraction involves the objects being replaced by fingers to be counted, or by actions like finger tapping or nods of the head. Until the stage of working with abstract number facts is achieved, children will be hampered in their progress to more complex calculations.

Number facts

Among the many number facts that are established through practical activities, some will be particularly important in forming the basis upon which further arithmetic is built. Rapid recall of the number pairs that make ten (called *number bonds to ten* or *complements in ten*) will be crucial for later calculations and these form important 'benchmarks' that children will refer to constantly. In the initial stages of calculating, confident recall of these number facts will be more important than any formal recording. Different resources will be helpful in providing visual imagery to support the association of number pairs. A bead string with ten beads in two colours (see Chapter 1) can be given to each child who can then rearrange the beads to show different number pairs. Arranging the beads into fives makes number recognition easier (for example 6 is seen as 5 and 1 more) and may be associated with the fingers on each hand (Figure 4.2).

Figure 4.2   6 is 5 and 1 more.

Children are also able to relate the facts they know to new calculations and when they know 2 add 3 they have the potential to relate this knowledge to '*two* hundred add *three* hundred'. Young children revel in the experiences of working with very large numbers and these applications help them to understand that mathematics involves a pattern of related ideas. Because of the language we use, extension is not so clear for the decade numbers and written recording may help to extend the pattern to '20 add 30'.

Adding to the decade numbers is also important for instant recall, for example '40 add 3' or '100 add 3', and it is notable that these are easy to verbalize but more difficult to record. When the children are secure with oral work, discussion can be introduced of how the resulting numbers can be recorded.

Progression in counting strategies for subtraction

For subtraction, Carpenter and Moser (1983) note a progression in stages similar to those they identify for addition. These are illustrated for finding $9 - 3$:

- 'count out' where the child may count out 9 fingers, lower 3, and count those remaining;
- 'counting back *from*', where the child counts from the larger number, 9, as many counted number words as the smaller number – '9 ... 8, 7, <u>6</u>';
- 'counting down *to*' where the backward count goes from the higher number down to the smaller number – '9 ... 8, 7, 6, 5, 4, 3', tallying to get the answer <u>6</u>;
- 'count *up*' from 3 to 9;
- 'using known facts and derived facts'.

These different approaches are sometimes evident in children's finger methods – in the calculations '9–2' and '9–7', for example, where the most effective strategies would be 'counting down from 9' (9 ... 8, <u>7</u>) and 'counting down to 7' (9 ... 8, 7) respectively. Although the words and actions may be exactly the same in these two finger methods (try them for yourself!) the solutions relate, in the first case to the *last number spoken*, '7', and in the second to the *number of words uttered* between 9 and 7. It is easy to underestimate the understanding shown, and even the children themselves may not realize the different methods they are using. Watching children will help teachers assess the strategies they are using. Sharing discussion of their explanations will give children opportunities to broaden their own range of calculating strategies.

At this stage, developing number sense involves *meta-cognition* as children reflect on some of the answers to problems and find connections. Some children will realize for themselves that 9 − 7 may equally well be solved using an addition strategy (counting from 7 to 9) but others will need this idea to be pointed out explicitly and they will need to see the ways addition and subtraction relate in practical situations. It is not only the numbers 9, 7 and 2 that are related but the operations themselves that are 'inverse operations', operations that work in reverse and involve precisely the same number triple. The connection between addition and subtraction as 'inverse operations' can be explored using diagrams (Figure 4.3). Depending on which number or operation boxes are left blank this example can be used to focus on links that can be made. Blank diagrams may be filled in by the children who will also find it challenging to construct similar problems for each other.

Relating addition and subtraction

Associated with every addition fact there are two subtraction facts that are immediately available without the need for any calculation. If '5 and 3 together make 8' this also means that '8 is 3 more than 5' and '8 is 5 more than 3', or that '8 subtract 3 is 5' and '8 subtract 5 is 3'. Before isolating addition and subtraction in written recording, work can be done to identify *number triples* and to explore different ways of recording the findings diagrammatically and with numbers.

Many children who achieve early success in addition and subtraction do so by recognizing that what is required is the third number in such a number triple. This remains a powerful strategy and marks early differences between children who 'just know the answer' and those who continue to count. To develop number sense, teachers will need to make explicit reference to the way

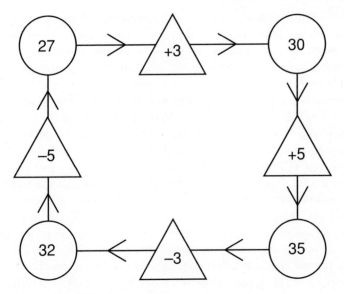

Figure 4.3 Diagrams to show + and − as inverse operations.

number triples can be used and the way new facts can be derived from those that are already known. As the easiest facts for children to remember appear to be the 'doubles' ('2 add 2', '3 add 3', '4 add 4' etc.), other numbers can be associated as 'near doubles'. For example, '5 add 6' can be identified as one more than 10, or '8 add 7' as one more than 14. Making this kind of link not only helps children to derive new facts from the ones they already know, but also helps to establish strategies for calculating. Rather than using a counting strategy, children should be encouraged to link new questions to any facts that they already know. Discussion of all the various approaches they suggest will help children become flexible in their approaches to problem solving and it can be fruitful to spend some time considering different approaches to a single problem rather than tackling several problems that are not connected.

Transforming problems and making connections

A powerful strategy for calculating is to transform the problem and use an easier procedure (or easier numbers) than those that are given. When children learn that $9 - 4$ can be solved by *adding* an appropriate number to 4, they can either use a counting on strategy, or a number fact $(4 + 5 = 9)$ to solve the problem. It is possible not only to change the procedure from subtraction to addition but also to change the numbers using a system of *compensation*. Knowing that $10 - 4$ results in 6, it may be immediately clear that $9 - 4$ gives one less. Underlying all calculations are the basic facts and, most importantly, the connections that children continue to establish about the way numbers relate to each other. Gray and Tall (1994) extend their idea of a procept to explain why children of differing abilities with apparently the same knowledge of number facts, solve addition and subtraction problems in different ways (see Chapter 3). To add $5 + 9$ can be a challenging task if you do not have the procept that 9 is $10 - 1$ (which in turn relates to the idea that 9 is the counting number before 10). They suggest the phrase 'slow learner' is a misnomer because the less able do not simply learn the same techniques more slowly but develop different techniques. Even the process of reversing addition to give subtraction is seen by the less successful child as a new process (counting back instead of counting up). The proceptual thinker is faced with a far easier task as counting, addition and subtraction are all operating with the same number procept, which allows numbers to be decomposed or reconstructed and used in related procedures for calculation purposes.

Recording addition and subtraction facts

When working with schemes or texts, addition and subtraction are sometimes introduced pictorially or diagrammatically with rapid progress to the symbols which are explained by the teacher. With repeated practice of particular procedures, many children may come to understand these operations as a particular 'ritual' that they do not associate with their wider experiences with numbers. In writing about current practices in the early years classroom, Carol Aubrey expresses concern that 'scheme work *determined* when and how addition and subtraction were introduced' (Aubrey, 1997, p. 23). Working from schemes, teachers work as mediators between their pupils and the text, and although children may learn how to do 'sums' in this way, the justification for particular methods of recording and the meanings of all the symbols are not made explicit.

The reason that the relationship between numbers such as 5, 3 and 8 is recorded as $5 + 3 = 8$ is not always clear to children. This result could equally well be written as $(5, 3) + = 8$ and read as '5 and 3 added together make 8'. This corresponds to the actions 'make a collection of 5 and a collection of 3 and put them together'. The answer relates to a particular convention, just as there is a convention about the way to spell a word like 'boat'. This is not the only possible way to record this result and it could equally well be symbolized as $8 = 5 + 3$ and read 'we found 8 when we added 5 and 3'. Difficulty with the 'equals' sign will arise if it is always seen to precede the answer and is interpreted as 'makes'. Early recording needs to involve a variety of formats to show how symbols can be used and interpreted in a variety of ways.

If children are to focus on the numerical results, flexibility in recording will need to be introduced from the earliest stages and patterns in the numerical results made the focus of attention:

$$8 = 5 + 3$$
$$8 = 6 + 2$$
$$8 = 7 + 1$$
$$8 = 8 + 0$$

Another purpose for recording will be to establish patterns that will enable children to derive new results from those that are already known (Figure 4.4). An attractive wall display can be made where children share and compare their findings while all working at their own level.

Reading the symbols

Symbolic representation will be used to ask questions as well as for recording findings. This may help to establish links between a variety of questions involving the same number triple. Children will need to use and understand some complex mathematical language when 'reading' or 'putting into words' the relationships in 'missing

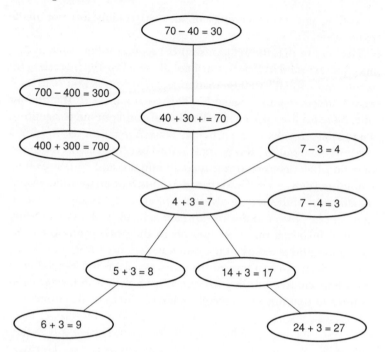

Figure 4.4   A web of results derived from $4 + 3 = 7$.

number' problems as such problems can help to establish that symbols can be interpreted in flexible ways. Consider the following examples:

$3 + \square = 8$	$\square + 3 = 8$	$3 = 8 - \square$

$5 = \square - 3$	$\square - 5 = 3$	$8 = 5 + \square$

In attempting to 'read' the symbols, some expressions will be more difficult to verbalize than others. The expression '$8 - \square$' may be related to a set of 8 objects from which some are removed, while '$\square - 3$' represents a situation which may be referred to as 'start unknown'. Those who understand the relationship between 3, 8 and 5 may *know* the answer; otherwise a 'trial and improve' strategy may be used for children who are stuck. A question such as 'Could it be 4?' will sometimes help individuals to work from some of the facts that they already know. 'Will the number be bigger than 4 or smaller than 4?' will not only help lead to a solution but will also provide a strategy of trying other numbers and making deductions from these findings – an important strategy in developing number sense. In such problems, the learning objective for children will be to establish ways of 'reading' the expressions and relating them to procedures. Teachers will need to be thoughtful in the ways they give support to those in difficulty without 'giving' them interpretations for these problems.

Problems presented in word form generate difficulties of a different kind. When all the words are given, the task becomes one of interpreting the meaning of the question and identifying it with an addition or subtraction procedure. Word problems will vary in their semantic structure and Dickson *et al.* (1984) identify different types of word problem that can be represented as $3 + 2 = 5$. They include such word problems as 'John has three large cars and two small cars. How many cars does he have altogether?' which they identify as the *union* aspect of addition. Alternatively, 'John has three cars. Jane has two more cars than John. How many cars does Jane have?' which is referred to as the *comparison* aspect of addition. Children's strategies for solving these two problems would probably be quite different, with the second presenting more difficulty than the first.

Carpenter and Moser (1983) give one of the most complete analyses of addition and subtraction word problems distinguishing classes of problems on the basis of their semantic structure. They identified four main types of problem: *change, combine, compare* and *equalize,* each with subclasses of addition and subtraction problems (see Table 4.1). They show that children's solution processes clearly reflect the structure of the problem as well as the numbers involved, with some presenting much more difficulty than others.

The *active, 'change'* problems involve a procedure within the problem, in contrast with the *passive, 'combine'* problems which suggest no procedure. Although the difference may appear to be subtle, the image of further marbles being 'given' suggests actions that could be used to find the result of the first problem, whereas the second has no such actions. Contrast these with the '*compare'*

Table 4.1 Four main types of addition and subtraction word problems

change	Mara has 5 marbles. Ben gives her 8 more marbles. How many does she have altogether?	Ben has 8 marbles and he gives 3 to Mara. How many does he have left?
combine/separate	Mara has 5 blue marbles and 8 red marbles. How many marbles does she have?	Together Ben and Mara have 13 marbles. If Ben has 5, how many does Mara have?
compare	Mara has 8 marbles and Ben has 5 marbles. How many more than Mara does Ben have?	Ben has 5 marbles. He has 8 fewer than Mara. How many does Mara have?
equalize	Mara has 8 marbles and Ben has 5 marbles. How many must Ben win to have the same as Mara?	Mara has 5 marbles. If Ben loses 8 marbles he will have the same number as Mara. How many does Ben have?

problem: 'Mara has five marbles. Ben has eight more than Mara. How many marbles does Ben have?'. This third problem is more difficult because the imagery it presents is much more complex and a third subset of marbles, or a complete set including all of Ben's, needs to be visualized. Although all of these problems can be symbolized by the expression '8 + 5 = 13', they relate to different representation including all the different missing numbers problems. For example, $\square - 8 = 5$ may be related to 'Ben has five marbles. He has eight fewer than Mara. How many does Mara have?'.

Teachers can help to develop their pupils' understanding by introducing a wide range of semantic structures and making these the basis for discussion. Although it is tempting to simplify the wording of a problem, or to give an alternative interpretation to children in order that the calculation can be attempted, this is a situation in which much of the mathematical learning relates to the words and meanings, rather than the arithmetic calculations. Children themselves should gain experience by making up word problems to match addition and subtraction calculations, and groups can work together to give a number of alternatives for any number problems they are given.

Working mentally with larger numbers

Counting on and counting back will help establish answers to various problems but this counting needs to be made progressively more efficient by introducing 'chunks' that relate counting to established number facts. Adding 7 and 3 to make 10, for example, should become an established 'benchmark' fact so that any number 'ending' in 7 is associated with the 'chunk' 3. Working with an 'empty number line' can help give a visual image that encourages progression from 'hops' that represent 'counting in ones' to 'jumps' using different 'chunks' that illustrate such known facts (Figure 4.5).

Figure 4.5   17 + 3 using a step of 3 on the empty number line.

Using known facts will provide an efficient strategy for working '*within decade boundaries*' but may not be quite so easily related to calculations that go '*across decade boundaries*'.

within decade boundaries	12 + 3 = 25 + 4 = 84 + 3 =
across decade boundaries	17 + 5 = 25 + 6 = 84 + 8 =

It will be possible to use the 'benchmark' facts involving the number bonds for ten for the latter of these types of problem using a strategy sometimes referred to as 'bridging to ten'. This involves partitioning the number to be added so that the first 'chunk' takes the total to a decade number and then the remaining units are added (Figure 4.6).

Adding by 'bridging to ten'

17 + 5 =	17 + 3 + 2 = 20 + 2
25 + 6 =	25 + 5 + 1 = 30 + 1
84 + 8 =	84 + 6 + 2 = 90 + 2

Figure 4.6 'Bridging to tens' on an empty number line.

Another 'benchmark' in children's understanding relates to their understanding of the effect of starting at any number and adding ten. This should be automatic for children before two-digit addition and subtraction are introduced and those who do not *know* that 24 add 10 gives 34 will need to spend more time with calculators, bead strings or 'tens' and 'units' structured apparatus to establish these patterns of results. In the chapter on counting, the idea of 'counting on ten' was introduced with the idea of a 'tens catcher' that provides a visual image of the resulting pattern of numbers. Once ten can be added to any number, the empty number line can be used to record results and multiples of ten can be introduced. Three 'jumps' of ten can be replaced by the quicker 'jump' of 30 all in one go (Figure 4.7a).

For certain calculations, particularly those involving numbers that end in 1 or 2, or 8 or 9, an easier calculation is possible by changing the calculation using a procedure sometimes referred to as '*compensating*'. Adding 28, for example, can be achieved by adding 30 and subtracting 2 from the result. On the number line, this corresponds to a 'jump' forward of 30 and a 'jump' backwards of 2 (Figure 4.7b).

Mental methods for adding and subtracting two two-digit numbers

Mental strategies for adding or subtracting two two-digit numbers fall into two main categories: *sequence methods* and *split tens methods*

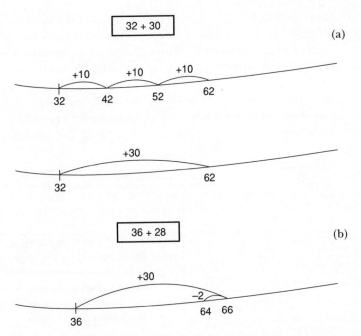

Figure 4.7 (a) Empty number lines with three jumps of 10 and one jump of 30.
(b) Adding 28 by going forward 30 and back 2.

according to whether they are related to 'counting' or to 'place value'. *Sequence methods* retain one number as a whole and partition the other into convenient 'chunks' to add or subtract. *Split tens methods* partition both numbers into tens and units. Some of the different ways to 'think about' the addition calculation 27 + 35 can be represented in the following ways:

Sequence methods	Split tens methods
27 + 35 = (27 + 30) + 5	27 + 35 = (20 + 30) + (7 + 5)
27 + 35 = (27 + 3) + 2 + 30	27 + 35 = (7 + 5) + (20 + 30)
27 + 35 = (20 + 35) + 7	
27 + 35 = (35 + 5) + 22	Compensation method
	27 + 35 = (25 + 2) + (25 + 10) = 50 + 12

It is notable that mental split tens methods retain the wholeness of the numbers so that a number such as 27 may be regarded as '20 and 7' rather than '2 tens and 7 units'. The latter is introduced in the very curtailed written algorithms that will be discussed in Chapter 6.

These same approaches may form the basis for subtraction strategies. Some of the different ways to 'think about' the subtraction calculation $45 - 27$ can be represented in the following ways:

Sequence methods	Split tens methods
$45 - 27 = (45 - 20) - 7 = 25 - 7$	$45 - 27 = (40 + 5) - (20 + 7) =$ $(30 + 15) - (20 + 7) = (30 - 20)$ $+ (15 - 7)$
$45 - 27 = (45 - 5) - 20 - 2 = 40$ $- 20 - 2$	$45 - 27 = (40 + 5) - (20 + 7) =$ $(40 + 15) - (30 + 7) = (40 - 30)$ $+ (15 - 7)$ this method, known as 'equal additions', used to be the most commonly taught algorithm
$45 - 27 = (47 - 27) - 2$ a 'transformation' method	

This subtraction calculation can also be effectively related to addition and undertaken by 'counting on' from 27 to 45 and all the experiences of addition methods can be used in mental methods for subtraction. An efficient example is the following:

From 27 to 47 is 20, so from 27 to 45 is 2 less, that is 18.

Fuson *et al.* (1997) suggest a similar classification of strategies in their references to three classes of methods used for addition and subtraction of two-digit numbers. They identify these methods for the calculations $38 + 26$:

- **'sequence methods'** such as counting on by tens and ones e.g. begin with one number and move up or down the sequence by tens or ones e.g. 38, 48, 58, 59, 60, 61, 62, 63, 64;

- **'collected multiunit methods'** in which the tens and then th ones are counted or added e.g. 30 and 20 is 50; 8 and 6 is 14, now add 50 and 14 to get the answer 64;
- **'concatenated single digits'** in which the numbers are used as strings of digits e.g. 8 and 6 is 14, which gives four units and one ten to 'carry', 3 and 2 is 5 with the one carried forward makes 6 to get 6 . . . 4 as the answer.

This last method is usually associated with a vertical layout where the children add or subtract separate columns. Whereas the first two methods deal at all stages with the whole numbers, retaining their values, the third deals with the digits only and it is the positioning in a written calculation that gives them their value. These methods are not always used separately but may be mixed, for example, with tens added or subtracted and then a sequence method used to add or subtract the remaining ones. For example, to calculate 38 + 26 as a combination of 'chunking' and counting in ones: 30 and 20 is 50, 50 and 8 is 58, 59, 60, 61, 62, 63, 64. Fuson *et al.* (1997) also identify the 'transformation' method in which both numbers are changed to make an easier calculation: for example, 38 and 26 gives the same total as 40 add 24.

Thompson (1997) uses different category names but identifies broadly the same categories in his analysis of the mental strategy used by children:

- *'cumulative sum'* starts with one number (most efficiently the largest one), increases this number by the appropriate multiple of ten and then adds the units either by counting on or by using complements in 10, e.g. 38, 48, 58 and 2 makes 60 and then 4 more make 64;
- *'partial sums'* works separately with the 'tens' and 'units';
- *'cumulo-partial sums'* initially adds the tens and then uses this new number as the start for a cumulative method.

Thompson suggests that children who are not taught formal written methods will develop their own, often idiosyncratic, methods and suggests different layouts for written recording that can 'match' the child's individual approach. These will be discussed in Chapter 6.

₁977) suggests that mistakes associated with written ̣ds are often based on rules that have been misapplied, for ̣xample always subtracting the smaller digit from the larger in subtraction. These are more likely to occur where children are trying to follow rules they have learned without adequate under-standing. Where procedures for calculating have been 'given' to children, they can see arithmetic as an arbitrary game of following rules, with the answers depending on the rules you follow. Teachers sometimes worry about allowing children to discuss their own approaches to a problem in case wrong ideas are suggested. Their inclination is always to ask children who are likely to be correct in their explanation of their methods. Research, on the other hand, shows that learning is more effective when common misconcep-tions are exposed, addressed and discussed in teaching (Askew and Wiliam, 1995, pp. 12–13). Drawing attention to a misconception before giving the examples is less effective than letting the pupils fall into the 'trap' and then having the discussion. It seems that to teach in a way that avoids creating *any* misconceptions (sometimes called 'faultless communication') is not possible and many miscon-ceptions will remain hidden unless the teacher makes specific efforts to uncover them. Addressing misconceptions during teach-ing does actually improve achievement and long-term retention of mathematical skills and concepts.

CHAPTER 5

Multiplication and Division

When children initially develop strategies for multiplication and division they already know about addition and subtraction and will begin by relating each new operation to things they already know. Early experiences will not involve the mathematical symbols but will need to introduce a range of practical situations that will help to establish meanings for the vocabulary associated with the operations. Words like 'multiply' and 'divide' are not often found in everyday conversation but will formalize a variety of words that are used to describe multiplicative situations, such as 'lots of', 'each', 'times' and 'share'.

Greer (1992) identifies four main categories of practical situation that involve the multiplication of whole numbers:

- equivalent groups (e.g. three tables, each with four children);
- multiplicative comparison (*scale factor*) (e.g. three times as many boys as girls);
- rectangular arrays (e.g. three rows of four children);
- cartesian product (e.g. the number of different possibilities for girl–boy pairs from three girls and four boys).

Each of these situations can be associated with particular ways of asking a question, and each may be represented in a way that shows *repeated sets, many-to-one* correspondence, an *array* of rows and columns, and a *many-to-many* correspondence, respectively (Figure 5.1).

These situations all involve three numbers in a mathematical relationship: the number of objects in each set, the number of sets and the total number. For multiplication it is the total number that is missing but if either of the other two numbers is to be found, division is introduced. For division, either the number of groups, or

Figure 5.1 *Repeated sets*, a *many-to-one* correspondence, an *array* of rows and columns, and a *many-to-many* correspondence.

the number in each group, can be missing. It is therefore possible to identify two distinct types of division:

- measurement/grouping (*quotitive*) (e.g. twelve children at tables of four, how many tables?);
- sharing (*partitive*) (e.g. twelve children at four tables, how many at each?).

It will be important for children to think about multiplication and division in all these different ways and to appreciate that they may all be related to the same numerical calculations. Although each of the situations above suggests actions that could be used to solve a problem, it is the understanding of abstract relationships between numbers that will encourage efficient approaches. It is then that children will realize that a calculation procedure does not need to reflect the structure of the problem to be solved.

Early experiences

Although multiplication is introduced first in school, the actions of sharing and grouping are probably more familiar. Research has shown that children as young as four years old are capable of performing dividing procedures in some situations with concrete materials (Pepper and Hunting, 1998). As early as kindergarten, children can model both grouping and sharing division problems with objects (Carpenter *et al.*, 1993; Kouba, 1989). The process of formalizing these ideas involves the introduction of precise language and a focus on the number relationships that are generated. Nunes and Bryant (1996) distinguish between the *action* of sharing and the *operation* of division, because understanding division involves a diversity of situations beyond the actions of sharing. In contrast to sharing, removing equal groups from a set of objects more directly shows that repeated subtraction breaks down a set, reversing the way multiplication builds up a set from equal groups.

Nunes and Bryant (1996) suggest that the simplest form of multiplicative situation that children will meet is probably one in which there is a *one-to-many correspondence* between two sets (e.g. one car with four wheels) which relates to a *ratio*, or *scale factor*, and is the basis for multiplicative, rather than additive thinking. They contrast this with *repeated addition*, which they refer to as *replicating* and

69

suggest that replication is not like *joining* (for addition) where any two sets of objects can be combined to give a new set of the same types of objects. Multiplication relates to two numbers, each having a different role (the number in each set and a tally for the number of sets), which needs to be co-ordinated in a way that is more complex than addition. Collecting five sets of four wheels will require each set of four objects to be counted as individual items *and* the same objects collected into sets as the sets themselves are counted.

Early experiences involve children in learning to count sets as well as counting individual objects. Partitioning and regrouping objects in equal sets will help to establish the language and numerical relationships that will be the foundation for later calculations. Even where children work confidently with numbers, the abstraction needed to appreciate the way three numbers relate in multiplication and division is not as immediately clear as the relationship generated when two sets are combined in addition. Gray and Tall (1994) suggest that the introduction of multiplication and division can present a 'proceptual divide' between those who can and cannot integrate these new ideas within their existing understanding. They note that there can be a cumulative effect of new operations, and multiplication and division ideas will be almost impossible for some children to co-ordinate while they are having problems with addition and subtraction.

Number patterns and inverse operations

Links between the different arithmetic operations can be established by expressing the same results in different ways. 'Two add two add two' can be expressed as 'three lots of two' or 'three times two'. By asking the question 'How many lots of two make six?' the idea of division is introduced as the inverse of multiplication. These ideas are related to counting in twos, '2, 4, 6', and fingers can be used to keep a tally to show that 6 is 'three lots of two'. Getting children to extend these ideas to 'four lots of two' and 'five lots of two' by counting in twos and tallying with fingers will provide a mental strategy that is helpful for calculating and which will help them to be less reliant on manipulating the actual materials. Fingers will continue to be a valuable resource to aid the memory in the more complex thinking needed for multiplication and division.

With such small numbers it is not always clear to children that multiplication is introducing a new and powerful operation and some will continue to rely on addition to solve problems. When large numbers are introduced, such as the multiples of 20, the distinction between '3 add 20' and '3 lots of 20' introduces a bigger contrast that can illustrate more clearly that multiplication is a distinct operation for recording.

Remainders

In their experiences children will find that some numbers will not relate quite so neatly to equal groupings, for example seven objects cannot be grouped exactly in twos and will involve objects that are 'left over'. This can be the focus for discussion as 'seven is not in the pattern of counting in twos' or 'seven is only one more than six', as number sense is developed to reason about the numbers involved. Rather than isolating multiplication and division, connections between the numbers and the operations will help develop the 'feel' for numbers that is so important. Ask any adult what happens when thirteen objects are to be shared between four people and there will be no need to refer to any sharing procedure as thirteen is a familiar number that is easily related to twelve, which is a multiple of four. Such familiarity with numbers will develop when children progress from practical activities to talking about and recording relationships among the numbers.

Learning the patterns

From counting in twos, fives and tens (sometimes referred to as 'skip' counting) children can be encouraged to learn the number patterns for other numbers, including multiples of 20, 100 or 15, extending them as far as they can. Stages in developing such patterns take children from counting every one, to internalizing the interim numbers, and then using only multiples. Through ideas of equal groupings, children develop new counting patterns where some numbers are emphasized more than others (e.g. 1, 2, 3, 4, 5, 6, 7, 8, 9 ...). This involves a concurrent count as each triple of numbers is monitored and a *rhythm* is very helpful to maintain the pattern of three each time. Where children are using this strategy to calculate a given multiple, say six threes, a third concurrent count will be needed to tally the number of threes and children can sometimes be seen using their fingers to keep this tally (see Chapter 2). The interim numbers are then left out altogether (3, 6, 9 ...) and knowing this counting pattern already reduces to two the concurrent counts that need to be kept. Knowing these counting sequences is not yet enough for understanding multiplication and division but it brings familiarity to 'families' of numbers and rapid recall of such patterns will be helpful in later calculations.

It is very powerful, where multiplication and division are concerned, to have a 'sense' that the number 16 relates well to 2 and 4 and 8, but not so well to 5 or to 3. Teaching number sense involves helping children to understand that multiplication and division can both be related to the same number patterns and that it is these number relationships that will provide the ultimate key to successful calculating.

Diversity in meanings

The situations identified above all relate to whole numbers and this is the way the operations will first be introduced. In developing number sense, identifying multiplication only as repeated addition, and division only as sharing, will impose limitations for children by making the interpretation of some later calculations impossible, for example, 0.3×0.4 and $12 \div \frac{1}{2}$. In order to extend the meanings to include these types of calculation, the idea of a *ratio* between pairs of numbers is used, for example with pattern of numbers 0, 1, 2, 3, ... associated with 0, 4, 8, 12, (4 times). This type of ratio can be developed to reflect relationships between numbers that are not integers, for example 0, 1, 2, 3, ... associated with 0, 0.2, 0.4, 0.6, ... (Figure 5.2).

Using this idea of a ratio, multiplying by a number smaller than one can be identified with division, for example, finding one third of a group of twelve by dividing by three. Alternative representation will be associated with the idea of a *ratio* of two numbers when equivalent fractions are discussed in Chapter 7.

Figure 5.2 Number lines showing '4 times' and '0.2 times'.

Introducing the multiplication symbol

The multiplication symbol can be introduced as a succinct way of writing repeated addition and, as such, will be a welcome shorthand for recording some of the facts that children have known for some time. Although multiples of two are usually the first family of facts to be introduced, the real value of the shorthand notation is not immediately obvious ($2 + 2$ is little different from 2×2) and confusion is quite common. Greater motivation for the new symbol can be achieved if its efficiency is clearer, and starting with multiples of 25 can be fun, as well as giving purpose for using the new symbol.

Confusion can also develop about the way multiplication is written, as 3×25 and 25×3 are often interpreted in exactly the same way. It is sometimes argued that the 'correct' way of reading 3×25 is '3 multiplied by 25', that is, 'three taken twenty-five times' or $3 + 3 + 3 + \ldots + 3 + 3$. This fits with the other operations where addition, subtraction and division 'operate on' the first number with the second but flexibility in interpretation will lead to sensible choices.

The 'everyday' interpretation of 3×25 as '3 times 25', that is, twenty-five taken three times or $25 + 25 + 25$, may be more sensible in this case for calculating purposes. The word 'times' provides an appropriate alternative to 'multiplied by' as long as teachers are aware that hesitation by children may arise from the ambiguity involved. What is important is that children are able to make appropriate choices in identifying a meaning for the symbols and a procedure for calculating. This can be shown in the alternative interpretations of expressions such as 2×50 (2 lots of 50) and $\frac{1}{2} \times 4$ (4 lots of $\frac{1}{2}$).

The commutative rule

The reason that different verbal interpretations are equally valid is the *commutative rule* which says that $2 \times 50 = 50 \times 2$, both giving the same numerical result. Since the images of '50 lots of 2' and '2 lots of 50' are quite different, and their equivalent representations as repeated addition give no clue to the reason why they are equal, it may take some time for children to use the commutative rule effectively.

$$50 + 50 = 2 + 2 + 2 + 2 + 2 + 2 \ldots \text{fifty times}$$

Research has shown that experiences of repeated addition, particularly where there are images of repeated sets, impose limits on developing mathematical ideas involving commutativity (Schlieman *et al.*, 1998). Working with street vendors with little schooling and with school pupils, they found that specific teaching plays an important role in developing the ability to use commutativity in solving multiplication problems. Nunes *et al.* (1993) showed that even 9- and 10-year-old school children did not easily accept the commutative rule when they tried to solve context problems, such as calculating '14 lots of 3 dollars'. The structure of equal groups within the problems was influential in determining what number was to be repeatedly added. The commutative rule is important in establishing the flexibility needed to find the most efficient calculation strategy for any given problem.

One of the ways that the commutative rule can be investigated as a more abstract principle is by using an *array* and providing children with opportunities to arrange and re-arrange sets of objects (Figure 5.3).

Figure 5.3 An array showing '5 lots of 3' and '3 lots of 5'.

Moving objects into rows and columns will provide better opportunities to explore the commutative rule than static pictures which are sometimes difficult to see in the two different ways (as rows of one number, and at the same time columns of another number). Acceptance of the commutative rule marks progression from understanding multiplication only as repeated addition, to multiplicative approaches that relate to other types of problem: *scale factor* problems (e.g., a bicycle travelling eight times as fast as a pedestrian) and *cartesian product* problems (e.g., the number of sandwiches that can be selected using three types of bread and four types of filling). Both problems involve multiplication that is not so evidently repeated addition (Murray *et al.*, 1991; Mulligan and Mitchelmore, 1997).

Introducing the division symbol

As with multiplication, the division symbol may be introduced as a shorthand way of recording results already known, but the way to interpret the division symbol can cause difficulties that may not be evident in the earlier stages. The problem '600 ÷ 6' can be interpreted as 'how many lots of 6 make 600?' related to the count 6, 12, 18, ... or can be interpreted as '6 lots of what make 600?' which may lead to an easier solution. These interpretations may be identified with the 'repeated subtraction' and 'sharing' and show the importance of children being flexible in their interpretation of division. The interpretation of a problem such as $8 ÷ \frac{1}{4}$ will be virtually impossible if the only interpretation is one of sharing (8 shared by $\frac{1}{4}$ – of a person?). Children who do not have the flexibility to match an appropriate interpretation to a symbolic problem will be hampered in their progress to these calculations. Division does not obey the commutative rule although many children will attempt to use it when they meet a problem such as $4 ÷ 8$ (Anghileri, 1998). Early introduction to problems such as '4 shared between 8' in practical situations, discussing its contrast with '8 shared between 4', will show that smaller numbers *can* be divided by bigger ones, avoiding the misconception that 'division always makes smaller' (Fischbein *et al.*, 1985).

Reinforcing the importance of number triples

The most effective ways of calculating will become established when children recognize that multiplication and division both determine a number triple which may be identified independently of any practical procedure. The number 24, for example, is related to 3 and 8 in a way that involves both multiplication and division. This is reinforced by using the terms *factors* to identify two numbers that are combined by multiplication to give the result, which is called the *product*.

---

24 has 3 and 8 as two of its *factors*

24 is the *product* of 3 and 8

This relationship is expressed in four ways using the symbols '×' and '÷'

$3 \times 8 = 24$ $8 \times 3 = 24$ $24 \div 3 = 8$ $24 \div 8 = 3$

The term *divisor* of a number is an alternative to 'factor' used to identify any whole number that divides exactly into it without a remainder, for example 1, 2, 3, 4, 6, and 12 are all the factors/ divisors of 12. A corresponding term is the *multiple* of a number which refers to any numbers obtained by multiplication, for example 6, 9, 12 . . . are all multiples of 3. By recording multiplication and division facts together, and relating results to number patterns, children will gain a better sense not only of the number relationships that are involved with a number and its factors, but also the relationships that exist between the operations.

Learning the facts

Traditionally, learning 'times tables' has taken up a considerable amount of time in the primary school. For some children this is an efficient way for them to achieve immediate recall of those isolated facts that they will need when calculating. For other children, however, the task of memorizing so many facts becomes unmanageable, and alternative strategies must be found for enabling them to calculate rapidly. Not only are the facts difficult to memorize, but the isolation sometimes imposed by learning 'times tables' can inhibit children in using multiplicative methods to solve problems. Even in the later years in primary school some children persist with very primitive methods like tallying and repeated addition to calculate with large numbers (Anghileri, 1999b) where they are unsure of the ways multiplicative facts can be applied.

Chanting and rote learning can be helpful for learning some of the facts, and most children will be successful in learning the 'zero' and 'one times tables' which both hold important initial facts. Alternatively, the identification of patterns on a 100 square, will provide visual images that can help them to reconstruct those facts that are not immediately remembered (Figure 5.4).

Figure 5.4 Multiplication patterns on a 100 square.

The most important aspect of learning multiplication facts is the way each fact is related to a whole lot of others. Knowing '3 fours are 12', for example, should give rapid access to '6 fours' by doubling. As it appears to be easier to recall '7 sevens' than '8 sevens', adding one more seven onto 49 will be a better strategy than reciting the whole 'table' in the hope of jogging the memory. Making connections among the facts will not only minimize the number of facts to be learned but will encourage strategies that will reduce the working in later calculations (Figure 5.5). Doubling and halving are important preparations and, as soon as a few facts are learned, the emphasis can be transferred to all the connected facts that can be derived.

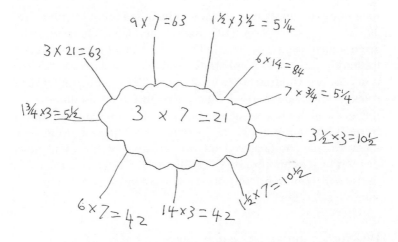

Figure 5.5 A web showing results connected with 3×7.

When the commutative rule is known, the number of facts to be learned is immediately halved. *Understanding how to make links is as important as memorizing the facts.*

Counting in twos, threes or fives is too often dismissed as irrelevant to classroom practice but children are often familiar with such patterns of numbers and they are important for developing number sense. They will provide a strategy for calculating that extends well beyond the limited facts in the 'tables' and chanting in 'fives', for example, shows a clear pattern in the numbers up to and beyond 100. Where a tally is kept (often with fingers) children have rapid access to a means of calculating with which they are secure and confident. Extending the counting pattern of twos to the patterns for four (only say every other number) will reinforce the connections and provide another access to number facts. Immediate access to as many multiplication and division facts as possible is desirable (for example, $3 \times 15, 4 \times 25$) but undue emphasis on 'times tables' will not achieve the aim of getting children to use these facts appropriately.

Extending the multiplication and division facts to multiples and powers of ten

Extending the multiplication facts to include multiples of ten (20, 30 ...) and powers of ten (100, 1000 ... and later 0.1) needs to be given some meaning as these will be an important part of strategies for multiplying larger numbers. Careful development of such ideas is necessary if children are to work with understanding rather than rules they have memorized. Multiplying by ten or one hundred is not a case of 'adding noughts' (this will fail when 0.5 is multiplied by ten!) but can be explained by repeated addition and the commutative rule, or explored on a calculator. At the same time, division by tens and hundreds can be related to these facts, using the idea that multiplication and division are inverse operations that 'undo' each other.

Developing understanding in stages

To retain understanding while developing ideas involving multiples and powers of ten, a variety of contexts are needed, such as working with money, measures, structured apparatus and calculators. This will introduce imagery that can help children to make sense of the abstract calculations. Ideas can be extended, progressively introducing some of the rules of arithmetic. The following possible stages are illustrated for 40×3, 400×3 and 40×30.

Stage 1: Using repeated addition and the commutative rule

Initially, $10 + 10 + 10 = 30$ is identified with *3 lots of ten*, and this is associated with *10 lots of three*, both making 30. Now *3 lots of forty* with *40 lots of three* is identified with $40 + 40 + 40 = 120$ and can be written as $40 \times 3 = 120$ or as $3 \times 40 = 120$. At the same time this relates to $120 \div 30 = 4$ and $120 \div 4 = 30$. (Some children may like to see this verified with a simple calculator, keying in $3, +, +$ and pressing the '=' button 40 times. Appropriate questions such as

'Will the display show 50, or 100?' can make this an opportunity to become more familiar with multiples of 3.) Extending this idea, '400 lots of 3' is the same as '3 lots of 400' and is associated with the four calculations:

$$400 \times 3 = 1200$$
$$3 \times 400 = 1200$$
$$1200 \div 400 = 3$$
$$1200 \div 3 = 400$$

Stage 2: Linking known facts and using the associative rule

The *associative rule* allows the numbers to be paired in a different way and then combined by multiplication, for example, $3 \times (4 \times 10) = (3 \times 4) \times 10$. Using the idea that $\times 40$ is the same as $\times 4$ followed by $\times 10$, allows 3×40 to be calculated as $(3 \times 4) \times 10 = 12 \times 10$. When multiples of 100 are known, 3×400 can be calculated as $(3 \times 4) \times 100$.

Stage 3: Both numbers as multiples of ten

The calculation 30×40 can be thought of as 30 lots of 40 or 40 lots of 30 but repeated addition will be inefficient. Using the associative rule can involve known facts:

$$30 \times 40 = 30 \times (4 \times 10) = (30 \times 4) \times 10 = 120 \times 10 = 1200$$
or
$$30 \times 40 = (3 \times 10) \times 40 = 3 \times (10 \times 40) = 3 \times 400 = 1200.$$
Using both the associative and commutative rule the result can be calculated as
$$(3 \times 10) \times (4 \times 10) = (3 \times 4) \times (10 \times 10) = 12 \times 100$$

The equivalent division problems would give $1200 \div 30 = 40$ and $1200 \div 40 = 30$.

It cannot be over-emphasized that the power in calculating lies in appreciating the patterns that are generated in this way. Children need encouragement to explore different combinations of numbers including multiples and powers of ten, and to talk about their findings so that the results themselves become familiar and a result such as 12×100 is 'known' rather than calculated.

A calculator provides a quick and reliable way to observe patterns like the effect of multiplying by ten. Rousham (1999) describes an activity in which groups of children would write down a list of numbers of their choice ('your age, your door number ... a big number, a small number . . .') and look for any patterns they might find. He claims that the calculator makes the activity more powerful because of the range of numbers and quantity of results that can be seen.

> The entire number system is built into a calculator, place value parti-cularly, and by using it a lot, much incidental information about how numbers behave and are changed by the various operations is absorbed in a way that is qualitatively different from working with the printed page. (Rousham, 1999, p. 95)

Rousham goes on to talk of the 'fierce interest in patterns, numbers and how they behave' as the children had the opportunity to investigate more and more numbers and retain control of the ideas they explored. With the calculators they gained experiences with many different numbers and the way they are related using multi-plication and division. This provides more powerful strategies for calculating than procedures that are abstractions from manipulat-ing concrete materials.

Mental strategies for multiplying larger numbers

Multiplication of larger numbers involves 'breaking' the calcula-tion into smaller parts and there are many ways this may be done. Where repeated addition is inefficient, more efficient 'chunks' can be used without losing understanding of the fundamental idea. The multiplication 3×26, for example, could be calculated as '3 lots of 20 together with 3 lots of 6' or it could be '3 lots of 25 and 3 more' and each of these calculations relates to a different way of 'chunking' the number 26 to relate to already established facts. The strategies that allow a calculation to be re-organized can be recor-ded in 'jottings' and addressed explicitly in discussions. Children will develop effective approaches and appropriate mathematical language by contrasting and comparing their different approaches under the guidance of a teacher. The teacher's role will be to help them to organize their informal recordings and make explicit the rules and conventions that underpin effective approaches.

Formally, both of the approaches above use the *distributive rule* that enables a multiplication to be 'distributed' over the sum of two parts:

$$3 \times 26 = 3 \times (20 + 6) = (3 \times 20) + (3 \times 6) = 60 + 18$$

or

$$3 \times (25 + 1) = (3 \times 25) + (3 \times 1) = 75 + 3$$

(Children need to know these results but not the name for the rule.)

This particular calculation could also have been tackled using a doubling and halving strategy as $3 \times 26 = 6 \times 13$ which is '6 twelves and 6 more' and this would result in different jottings. Children may enjoy finding as many ways as possible to do such a calculation and different ways to record their findings with the emphasis on gaining efficiency and devising clear recording methods.

When two-digit numbers are to be multiplied by two-digit numbers, mental strategies may need to be supported with pencil and paper. At this stage children will benefit from discussions that introduce a variety of methods. Sometimes the structure of a problem may suggest an approach but the calculation may or may not reflect this structure. Take, for example, the problem 'For the school fete, 24 children will each make 16 cakes. How many cakes altogether?' Although the context suggests 24 lots of 16, the calculation 24×16 can be approached as 24 lots of 16 or as 16 lots of 24.

24 lots of 16	16 lots of 24
(20 lots of 16) + (4 lots of 16)	(10 lots of 24) + (6 lots of 24)
(24 lots of 10) + (24 lots of 6)	(16 lots of 20) + (16 lots of 4)

Multiplication by a two-digit number can be avoided altogether if this problem is transformed by doubling and halving:

$$24 \times 16 = 48 \times 8 = 96 \times 4 = 192 \times 2 = 200 + 180 + 4 = 384$$

Such a method demonstrates the way connections may be made between calculations when a standard approach to recording is delayed. Perhaps the most elegant solution to this particular problem would be using the 'fact' that $25 \times 16 = 400$ and then subtracting 16 from 400.

It is important for individual pupils to identify a way of thinking about how any problem may be tackled, and the stages that need to be recorded. Starting with 'long-hand' notes, explaining the method, and structuring some written recording, are all part of the development of understanding. Some pupils will work quickly towards concise ways to record their work but some may need time to work with extended forms of recording in order for steps in the calculation to be meaningful.

Division with numbers beyond the tables facts

In the same way that multiplication of bigger numbers involves choices about the way a problem may be tackled, the same is true for division. Depending on the way a calculation is interpreted, a problem such as 96 ÷ 4 is seen as sharing (96 shared between 4) or repeated subtraction (how many 4s in 96?). Both methods may be developed to greater efficiency where 'chunks' of increasing size can be related to known facts (Anghileri and Beishuizen, 1998). Dividing 96 by 4 may involve 'sharing' ten at a time into four sets until 80 of the 96 have been 'used', the remaining 16 giving a further 4 each, so that 24 each is the result (Figure 5.6).

Figure 5.6   96 ÷ 4 by sharing 10 at a time.

Using repeated subtraction, this calculation can also be done by 'chunking' the 96 into numbers that are associated with four e.g. 96 = 40 + 40 + 16, with '10 lots of 4' and '10 lots of 4' and then '4 lots of 4'. Recognizing that 80 and 16 are appropriate 'chunks' will lead to a more efficient calculation. The recognition of related 'chunks' for a calculation will often involve multiples of ten, for example 10 lots of 4, or 20 lots of 4, and will provide a strategy that will extend to any size divisor. Just as multiplication 'builds up' numbers in stages, division can be seen as 'breaking down' numbers in equivalent stages. In this way division is reinforced as the inverse operation to multiplication.

Division with two-digit divisors

For division by a two-digit divisor there are various methods including the traditional long-division algorithm which will be discussed in the next chapter. Pupils will need to decide on the most effective approach for each problem they meet and some calculations will be best undertaken with a calculator. In some types of problem, number sense will play an important role where children select an approach that best suits the numbers involved. Take, for example, the problem $64 \div 16$. This problem cannot easily be solved using a traditional algorithm but as a repeated subtraction (how many 16s are in 64?) the solution is easier. The fact that pupils are familiar with the numbers 64 and 16, and relate them with the numbers 4 and 8, will be helpful in suggesting a doubling or halving approach that can be used to solve the problem. Adults will recognize the greater complexity involved in calculating $63 \div 17$ even before any strategy is attempted. It is this 'feel' for numbers and the associations they evoke that makes the difference between children who are confident in their calculation methods and those who attempt only to follow procedures they have been taught.

Informal approaches and 'messy' working

When working within a context, the structure of a problem can influence the strategy used to find a solution. Although some children become able to select a method independent of the problem type, but which best suits the numbers, there is evidence that other pupils find it difficult to know what is the connection between the mathematics previously taught and the context of the problem (Clarke and Kamii, 1996). Rather than using number facts they have learned, to solve the problems effectively, these pupils fall back on inefficient methods such as tallying or counting in ones (Figure 5.7).

1256 apples are divided among 6 shopkeepers. How many apples will every shopkeeper get? How many apples will be left?

Figure 5.7   An inefficient method for calculating.

Children's jottings or personal records will give teachers insight into the way problems are approached and the extent to which individuals are abstracting an arithmetic operation from the reality of a given problem.

Doubling and halving are often seen in children's informal approaches and will lead progressively to more efficiency with teacher support. In using informal approaches, children are able to explore their understanding of a problem and bring to it the facts and strategies they think are relevant (Figure 5.8).

The range of different strategies this involves provides a good basis for discussion and the children's understanding may be

432 children have to be transported by
15-seater buses.
–How many buses will be needed?

Figure 5.8 Informal working for 432 ÷ 15.

enhanced by talking about their own methods and listening to others. Although the method illustrated lacks the efficiency of a standard algorithm it is clear that the solution is focused on the problem with the result interpreted to give a realistic answer. Where the calculation becomes purely mechanical, errors in working can result in bizarre answers that are not realistic solutions to the problem (Figure 5.9).

Research has shown that many pupils focus mainly on the mathematics, stop at the point of reaching an arithmetic solution and do not re-interpret their answer into the real context of the problem to check if it is appropriate. A balance has to be achieved between the abstraction that involves selection of the most efficient calculation method, and applications of calculating to real problems.

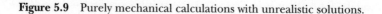

Figure 5.9 Purely mechanical calculations with unrealistic solutions.

CHAPTER 6

Written Calculations

Pencil and paper recording has been introduced in the previous chapters to support children's informal methods and to establish patterns in the relationships among numbers. This chapter will consider further developments to establish efficient written methods that children can understand and use successfully for numbers of increasing size and complexity.

In identifying the role of written procedures in a society that depends on technology for all important calculations, reservations about the need for *standard* algorithms have been expressed by mathematics educators for many years (Plunkett, 1979; Thompson, 1997; Anghileri, 1998). A strong view was expressed as long ago as 1979 by Stuart Plunkett:

> The advent of calculators has provided us with a great opportunity. We are freed from the necessity to provide every citizen with methods for dealing with calculations of indefinite complexity. So we can abandon the standard written algorithms, of general applicability and limited intelligibility, in favour of methods more suited to the minds and purposes of the users ... Children should be helped to acquire sensible methods for calculating ... [and] will acquire a better understanding of number from using their own mental algorithms than from the repeated application of standard algorithms they do not comprehend. (Plunkett, 1979, p.55)

In his classic article, Plunkett compares standard written methods of calculating with mental methods. He notes that standard written algorithms are *contracted, efficient, automatic, symbolic, analytic* and *generalizable*, but he points out the important disadvantage of the algorithms not being easily grasped by pupils because of their lack of correspondence with informal methods. Mental methods, on the other hand, are *fleeting, variable, flexible, active, holistic* and *constructive*, but overall, *personal* approaches for which the children have ownership. Teaching standardized procedures for calculating, he argues, encourages '*cognitive passivity*' and '*suspended under-*

standing' as they do not correspond to the way people naturally think about numbers. If the purpose of number work is to develop number sense then the contracted traditional algorithms, that rely on the manipulation of digits in a highly structured spatial arrangement, will be inappropriate for most calculations.

Although standard algorithms have been the focus for much teaching in the past, studies of workplace mathematics have also found that where pencil and paper methods are used by adults, these are rarely those methods traditionally taught in school (see, for example, the Cockcroft report, 1982, pp. 19–20). Rather than using formal written procedures, adults frequently use idiosyncratic jottings to support personal methods that are adapted to reflect the structure of the problem and the numbers that are involved. Teaching approaches need to acknowledge the way calculations are tackled 'in real life'. Also, as children have established foundations for calculating mentally it will be important to work progressively from the informal jottings that support mental strategies to more formalized methods so that their confidence and understanding are not jeopardized.

Children's intuitive approaches

Research has shown that, before standard methods are taught in school, children's first approaches to solving numerical problems reflect the understanding they have of each individual situation. Multiplication and division problems, for example, have proved to be interesting operations to study because children already have considerable experience with numbers that they bring to bear on any problem. In research on children's strategies for solving such problems, Mulligan and Mitchelmore (1997, p. 309) found that 'children acquire an expanding repertoire of intuitive models and that the model they employ to solve any particular problem reflects the mathematical structure they impose on it'. Even when the algorithms are introduced there is evidence that children persist in employing their own methods with better success. Murray *et al.* (1991) found that children

> invent powerful non-standard algorithms alongside school-taught algo-
> rithms: that they prefer to use their own algorithms when allowed to ...
> and that their success rate when using their own algorithms is sig-

nificantly higher than the success rate of children who use the standard algorithms or when they themselves use standard algorithms. (Murray *et al.* 1991)

From informal to formal written methods

The need for pencil and paper will arise where more complex calculations are introduced and some form of written recording is first developed to support mental calculation:

> Through a process of regular explanation and discussion of their own and other children's methods, [pupils] will begin to acquire a repertoire of mental calculation strategies. At this stage, it can be hard for them to hold all the intermediate steps in their heads, and so informal pencil and paper notes, recording some or all of their solutions, become part of a mental strategy. (DfEE, 1998, p. 109)

Such notes will start as unstructured personal jottings that may be difficult for a teacher or other pupils to decipher. 'These personal jottings may not be easy for someone else to follow, but they are a staging post to getting the right answer and to acquiring fluency in mental calculation' (DfEE, 1998, p. 109).

When larger numbers are involved, pencil and paper recording is necessary for keeping track of a calculation, and Ruthven (1998) identifies two distinct purposes: 'to augment working memory by *recording* key items of information' and 'to cue sequences of actions through *schematizing* such information within a standard spatial configuration'. The traditional methods that have been taught as algorithms (set procedures for written calculations) may provide the most succinct record, but their contracted form makes them beyond the capabilities of many children at primary school age.

Stages in a progression for written recording

Where written recording is introduced for a calculation, there are a variety of methods that follow a progression from mental to part-written, and then to more formally organized written methods that develop efficiency. It is important in the early stages of recording calculations not to introduce the vertical written format before children have had the opportunity to construct different recording methods for themselves. Although children may enjoy early success with algorithms, their contracted nature invites children to work with digits rather than the true values of the numbers and the more mechanical approach can be applied without understanding.

While the primary purpose for introducing the algorithms has been to 'direct and organize' children's approaches, their formal structure is prone to errors (Brown and Van Lehn, 1982). In analysing these errors it has been shown that children make inappropriate adaptations of the methods they learn as they try to reconstruct a procedure they have not understood and cannot remember. Ruthven and Chaplin (1998) refer to these types of error as 'the improvisation of malgorithms' suggesting that children appear to be following rules, but the wrong rules (Figure 6.1). In many cases the algorithms are difficult to understand as they do not relate to the children's intuitive approaches (Plunkett, 1979; Thompson, 1997; Anghileri, 1998; Anghileri and Beishuizen, 1998).

Independence from a standard approach will help children to develop confidence in using the number facts that they already know, in approaches that reflect the way they have interpreted the problems. In the early stages, their methods may be long-winded and inefficient but teachers will be able to help individuals to structure their written records and gain efficiency. By opening up discussion about the best ways to record the working for a given problem, children will gain experience in communicating their ideas both verbally and with the conventional symbols of mathematics. By developing the efficiency and organization of the children's own methods, understanding will not be sacrificed for the sake of efficiency and flexibility, and independent thinking will be encouraged so that appropriate methods may be selected for different problems.

Written methods: addition and subtraction

Mental strategies for addition and subtraction generally reflect two distinct mental approaches that have been described in Chapter 4: the *sequential methods* reflecting a counting approach and the *split tens methods* using place value. There are valid forms of formal recording associated with each of these approaches that can be progressively constructed to reflect the mental stages. If confusion is to be avoided, where a child is thinking of a solution strategy

1256 ÷ 6

Working

Answer....26....

64 ÷ 16

Working

Answer.6.1....r.1

432 ÷ 15

Working

Answer...21.r.2

1542 apples are divided among 5 shopkeepers.
How many apples will each shopkeeper get?
How many apples will be left?

Working:

Answer: 35 r 2
308

Figure 6.1 Errors with the division algorithm.

93

along the lines of one of these approaches, the form of written recording needs to reflect this thinking.

Sequential methods

In sequential methods one of the numbers is retained as a whole and subtotals are found by adding or subtracting parts of the other number. The most relevant recording starts with a horizontal arrangement that reflects the stages in a calculation.

$$58 + 37$$

$58 + 2 = 60$ $60 + 35 = 95$	or $58 + 30 = 88$ $88 + 2 + 5 = 95$

These mental methods can also be recorded on an empty number line that will illustrate steps in the procedure. It is arguable that the empty number line presents a highly efficient way to *record* any addition or subtraction calculation and may be the most easily understood by some children (Figure 6.2).

For subtraction there is the option of counting forwards from the smaller number or counting back from the larger. Again, these result in different written records:

$$57 - 38$$

$38 + 2 = 40$ $40 + 17 = 57$ so $57 - 38 = 17 + 2 = 19$	or $57 - 30 = 27$ $27 - 8 = 27 - 7 - 1 = 19$

These methods have the advantage that all stages in the process are transparent and build on children's knowledge of the ways numbers can be split into convenient 'chunks' so that known number facts can be used.

Split tens methods

Split tens methods involve the partitioning of both numbers and finding sub-totals based on place value. Initially it will be best for

Figure 6.2 Different methods for calculating 58 + 37 on an empty number line.

children to become familiar with a number such as 58 partitioned into '50 and 8' rather than '5 tens and 8 units' as discussed in earlier chapters. Just as the empty number line provides an image that will help children to visualize the sequential methods, there are images that can help illustrate split tens methods:

50		30		80
(58)	+	(37)	=	(95)
8		7		15

Thompson (1997) argues that to narrow the gap between children's idiosyncratic mental calculation methods and the traditional vertical written algorithms, first a holistic approach may be used that reflects more closely the actual quantities rather than work with digits. He identifies a partitioning algorithm that builds vertical recording on the mental strategy he refers to as 'a *partial sum* approach', using place value but working with whole numbers rather than digits:

95

```
        5 8
  +     3 7
        8 0
        1 5
        9 5
```

This procedure works from left to right, again reinforcing the way children may think about the problem. An alternative written method is suggested for children who use a 'cumulo-partial' approach:

```
        5 0
  +     3 0
        8 0
  +       8
        8 8
  +       7
        9 5
```

Again, this works with whole numbers and the recording shows all the stages involved. Each of these methods is rather more extended than the traditional algorithm but reflects more closely the mental methods that children are known to use. For some children it may be appropriate to move to more efficiency with part of the calculation done in the head, or with the small reminders, in the style of a traditional algorithm. The aids to memory may take many different forms and different options should be available according to those which are most easily understood by the children themselves:

```
      5 8          5 8          5 8           5 8
  +   3 7      +   3 7      +  ₁3 7       +   3 7
      9 5          9 5          9 5           9 5
      1 5          1                          10
```

It is important that children do not lose the sense in what they are doing and the reasonableness of the result for each calculation.

In a similar way to addition, Thompson suggests an expanded notation for subtraction:

$$
\begin{array}{rlll}
732 & 700+30+2 & \rightarrow & 600 + 120 + 12 \\
-\ 476 & -400+70+6 & & -\ 400 + \ \ 70 + \ \ 6 \\
\hline
256 & & & 200 + \ \ 50 + \ \ 6
\end{array}
$$

Unlike the addition methods, it will be necessary to work from left to right as the units introduce the immediate problem involved in subtracting a larger number (6) from a smaller number (2). There are many stages in this method which still do not appear explicitly and understanding will depend on individuals being confident to 'decompose' the number 732 as $600 + 120 + 12$. This is equivalent to the standard algorithm using decomposition but differs by keeping all the numbers whole rather than working with digits that have to be carefully aligned.

traditional decomposition algorithm:

$$
\begin{array}{rccc}
 & {}^6\cancel{7} & {}^{12}\cancel{3} & {}^1 2 \\
-\ & 4 & 7 & 6 \\
\hline
 & 2 & 5 & 6
\end{array}
$$

If children are to build on their established understanding of subtraction, then an approach that fits more readily with the mental strategies they have developed for smaller numbers would be to 'count up from 476 to 732' or to 'count down from 732 to 476'. Both of these may be recorded using an empty number line and it is arguable that this will be the most efficient written method for some children (Figure 6.3).

The question must be asked about what is the purpose of the calculation. As discussed in Chapter 1, if the purpose is to find the solution to a particular problem using an efficient and reliable method, then individual children should be encouraged to use any

Figure 6.3 An empty number line to show 732 − 476 by counting up and by counting down.

method that they are confident fits this requirement. On some occasions they may be encouraged to use a more traditional method that reflects the place value structure of the numbers. Whatever method is used, the objective should be made explicit and the choices available to the children made clear.

Thompson offers some more radical written methods as he notes that many successful mental methods begin by changing the problem to something that is easier and then adjusting the answer. He identifies a 'transformation' in which the problem 311 − 214 is solved mentally by first considering 314 − 214 and then subtracting 3 from the answer. In the example above, the calculation 732 − 476 could be undertaken by first subtracting 432 and then a further 44. In a similar manner, where a calculation such as 300 − 186 is problematic using the column arrangement of the standard algorithm, it is probably best solved using a counting on strategy from 186. A neat 'trick' for using the algorithm that children enjoy is to change the problem from 300 − 186 to 299 − 186 and then to add 1 to the result. These types of adjustment result in easier calculations and reflect valid mathematical thinking.

Using blocks to model a calculation

In the 1960s and 1970s structured materials like Dienes blocks, consisting of 'tens' rods and 'unit' cubes, were widely used to 'model' the traditional algorithms for addition and subtraction. The initial setting up of four tens and three unit blocks together with two tens and seven unit blocks for addition can be identified with the vertical written problem (Figure 6.4). (Using a large sheet of paper with the digits written on it and blocks placed on top can help children develop the imagery necessary.)

Comparing the steps for addition and subtraction reveals the way that modelling with blocks needs to be carefully 'orchestrated' and although the calculations 43 + 27 and 43 − 27 may look similar, the actions needed are quite different. Setting up the subtraction sum in the same way is not helpful where children identify subtraction with 'take away' because the two numbers that are represented by the blocks can only be compared. Reporting on a research study of children's understanding of the way blocks can be used to model addition and subtraction, Hart (1989, p. 139) claims that there is little connection as the blocks appear to give a model only for those who already understand the algorithm. 'Referring children to materials because they are having trouble ... is of little help unless one is sure that they have a workable method of setting up objects in order to mirror symbols.' She believes the gap between the two experiences is too large and children have great difficulty in making the connection. She showed that once children had been introduced to the written algorithm it was not long before they had completely forgotten any explanation. She summarizes the lack of connection between practical work and symbolic statements as 'Sums are Sums and Bricks are Bricks' (Hart, 1989, p. 139).

Introducing written methods for multiplication and division

Different contexts, particularly those that relate to the pupils' own experiences, are useful for generating multiplication and division problems, for example, costings for a class outing or cost per portion of different cereals. These will incorporate the important step of formulating the problem and identifying appropriate solution strategies, as well as interpreting the answer in a meaningful way. Collaboration on solving such problems may also generate

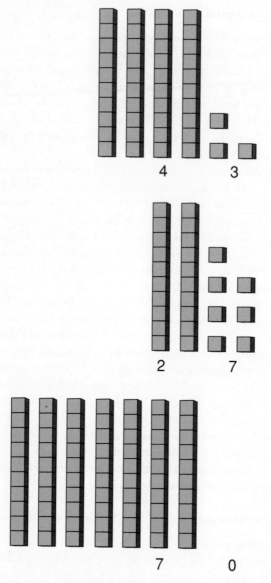

Figure 6.4 43 + 27 using blocks.

comparisons between mental, written and calculator strategies and introduce the choices that pupils need to be able to make.

   Motivation will be greater if the start for a calculation is a meaningful problem, such as 'If a person sleeps an average of 8 hours each night, how long does that person sleep in a year?' This multiplication of larger numbers involves 'breaking' the calculation into smaller parts. Repeated addition will become inefficient as the numbers get larger but this idea can be retained if pupils move progressively to more efficient 'chunks'. Doubling can also be a helpful strategy. There are many ways this may be done and partitioning using place value can be very effective. Written recording should express clearly the strategy used and children will need help to develop an organized format using mathematical symbols. A variety of approaches for calculating 365 × 8 can include 'messy working' that shows how the problem has been tackled.

$300 \times 8 =$ 2400 $60 \times 8 =$ 480 $5 \times 8 =$ 40 $365 \times 8 =$ 2920	$365 = 350 + 15$ $350 \times 8 = 700 \times 4$ $= 2800$ $15 \times 8 = 120$	365 doubled is 730 730 doubled is 1460 1460 doubled is 2920

$365 \times 8 = (400 \times 8) - (35 \times 8)$
$35 \times 8 = 35 \times 2 \times 4 = 280$
$400 \times 8 = 3200$
$3200 - 280 = 2920$
	365
	            ×8
	300×8 2400
	60×8 480
	5×8 40
	        2920

The 'rectangle' method is a good way to arrange a calculation based on chunking as it emphasizes the whole numbers rather than the digits:

	300	60	5
8	2400	480	40

The traditional 'long multiplication algorithm' is a highly efficient way to calculate but it has a very condensed form that makes it difficult to understand:

$$\begin{array}{r} 3\ 6\ 5 \\ \times 8 \\ \hline 2_2 9_5 2_4 0 \end{array}$$

Each time a multiplication of two digits gives a number greater than 9 (for example, $8 \times 5 = 40$), the 'tens part' must be 'carried forward' and added to the result of the next calculation (i.e. 4 must be added to the result of $8 \times 6 = 48$). The number to be 'carried forward' is usually written in small script in the column it will be added in and a considerable amount of working is done in the head. Because the contracted algorithm relies on steps that are not recorded it is important to keep expanded calculations as long as they are needed for sound understanding.

Two-digit multipliers

The problem above could also be calculated in two parts by noting that 8 hours a night gives $8 \times 7 = 56$ hours' sleep each week. Now the calculation for one year becomes 56×52 and the following recording methods relate to different approaches.

Different written methods for 56×52:

With jottings $100 \times 56 = 5600$ $50 \times 56 = 2800$ $2 \times 56 = 112$ so $52 \times 56 = 2800 + 112 = 2912$	Using doubling and halving $52 \times 56 = 104 \times 28 = 208 \times 14 = 416 \times 7$ Now $400 \times 7 = 2800$ $10 \times 7 = 70$ $6 \times 7 = 42$ and $2800 + 70 + 42 = 2912$

Rectangle method

	50	6
50	2500	300
2	100	12

So $56 \times 52 = 2500 + 300 + 100 + 12 = 2912$

Gelosia method

In the gelosia method the result is found by adding numbers diagonally to get 2 thousands, $(1 + 5 + 3)$ hundreds, $(0 + 1 + 0)$ tens and 2 units, i.e. 2912. The traditional algorithm may involve different stages, from an extended version that shows all the stages in the calculation, to the contracted version where much of the working is done mentally:

traditional	extended
56	
× 52	
12	6 × 2
100	50 × 2
300	6 × 50
2500	50 × 50
2912	

56	
× 52	
112	2 × 56
2500	50 × 50
300	50 × 6
2912	52 × 56

traditional
contracted
56
× 52
112
2800
2912

It is important that pupils retain flexibility in their approach so that they can use a method appropriate for the numbers involved. The problem 24 × 39, for example, can be tackled mentally if pupils can multiply 24 by 40. Sharing ways of thinking about calculations, and comparing ways to record working, will enable pupils to progress in their efficiency and develop understanding of the mathematical principles that underlie the different methods.

Multiplying a three-digit number by a two-digit number

When multiplying a three-digit number by a two-digit number, for example in the problem 'How many hours are there in 1 year?', the different stages of the calculation need to be recorded in an organized way and a vertical arrangement can be appropriate. Some pupils will prefer to work with the whole numbers at all stages while some may use doubling and halving.

With jottings
$300 \times 24 = 300 \times 12 \times 2 = 7200$
$60 \times 24 = 60 \times 12 \times 2 = 1440$
$5 \times 24 = 120$
$7220 + 1440 + 120 = 8760$
1 year is 8760 hours

Using doubling and halving
$365 \times 24 = 730 \times 12$
$730 \times 10 = 7300$
$730 \times 2 = 1460$
$730 \times 12 = 8760$
1 year is 8760 hours

Rectangle method

	300	60	5
20	6000	1200	100
4	1200	240	20

So $365 \times 24 = 6000 + 1200 + 100 + 1200 + 240 + 20 = 8760$ hours

traditional	extended
365	
$\times 24$	
6000	20×300
1200	20×60
120	24×5
240	4×60
1200	4×300
8760	

	traditional
	365
	$\times\ 24$
365×20	7300
365×4	1460
	8760

Making connections

It is often easier to calculate the multiple of a number starting with facts that are already known. Starting with any number and repeatedly doubling gives 2 times, 4 times and 8 times that number. Multiplying by 10 may also be recorded as a known fact. From these, all other multiples can be derived by adding. The calculation for 26 $\times$ 17 may be recorded in stages:

$$1 \times 17 = 17$$
$$2 \times 17 = 34$$
$$4 \times 17 = 68$$
$$8 \times 17 = 136$$
$$10 \times 17 = 170$$

Now $26 \times 17 = (10 \times 17) + (10 \times 17) + (4 \times 17) + (2 \times 17) = 170 + 170 + 68 + 34 = 442$

Since the same multiples, 2, 4, 8 . . . are used each time, a repertoire is developed of related facts about the way any number can be constructed from these powers of 2 (e.g., $26 = 20 + 4 + 2$).

Division with larger numbers and a single-digit divisor

Division problems can be interpreted in two ways relating to intuitive ideas of sharing or grouping. These ideas need to be reconciled with written recording, and informal jottings will help teachers to appreciate pupils' interpretation of problems. As noted in the last chapter, it can be helpful to identify division with repeated subtraction of 'chunks' and written recording can provide a structured record that will help children keep track. The calculation $96 \div 4$, for example, involves 'chunking' the 96 into numbers that are associated with four and a written record may be made in horizontal or vertical format:

<table>
<tr><td>

$96 = 40 + 40 + 16$
$= (10 \times 4) + (10 \times 4) + (4 \times 4)$
$= 24 \times 4$

</td><td>

$$
\begin{array}{rl}
96 & \\
-40 & \times 10 \\
\hline
56 & \\
-40 & \times 10 \\
\hline
16 & \\
-16 & \times 4 \\
\hline
0 & \times 24
\end{array}
$$

</td></tr>
</table>

The traditional algorithm is a very compact way to record a calculation but relies on precise first guesses and good understanding of the structure of a large number. Within the calculation, digits are used and children lose the values of the whole numbers. More long-winded recording allows pupils to reinforce their understanding of the process of repeated subtraction of chunks. For the traditional algorithm, on the other hand, pupils will need to be taught that '4 divided into 9' gives the 'tens' part of the answer and the remainder of 1 becomes 10 units. This is a shorthand for '4 divided into 90 gives 20 with 10 remaining'.

<table>
<tr><td>

$$
\begin{array}{r}
2\ \ 4 \\
4\overline{)9^16}
\end{array}
$$

</td><td>

Alternatively,
$96 = 100 - 4$ and $100 = 25 \times 4$
allows this calculation to be done
mentally!

</td></tr>
</table>

If pupils follow rules without understanding, errors will occur as the digits become the focus instead of the whole values of the numbers. Such a difficulty may arise when zeros need to be included in parts of the calculation and a common error occurs when they are omitted altogether:

$$6\overline{)1^125^56}\quad \begin{matrix}2\ 9\end{matrix}\quad \text{rem 2}$$

The following examples show some different written approaches for the calculation 1256 ÷ 6:

$$
\begin{array}{r}
6\overline{)1256} \\
600 \ \times 100 \\
\hline
656 \\
600 \ \times 100 \\
\hline
56 \\
54 \ \ \times 9 \\
\hline
\end{array}
$$

Answer 209 rem 2

1256 = 1200 + 56
1200 = 200 × 6
56 = 9 × 6 rem 2

Answer 209 with 2 left

$$6\overline{)1^12\ 5^56}\quad \begin{matrix}02\ \ 0\ 9\end{matrix}\ \text{rem 2}$$

Division with two-digit divisors

For division by a one-digit divisor there are various methods and the main advantage of a strategy based more explicitly on repeated subtraction is that the *same* method can be extended to work with two-digit divisors. The step from the traditional short division algorithm to long division, however, needs a re-organization of the written recording to include additional working. Written recording is most easily understood if it relates to the children's way of thinking about the problem. In developing written recording to introduce better efficiency, children can be encouraged to discuss and compare their approaches and the ways they write them down.

Working with problems in 'real' contexts may suggest approaches that use doubling, halving or multiples of ten. In the example, '432 school children are going on an outing. If each bus takes 15 passengers, how many buses will be needed?', efficiency can be gained by using 'chunks' of 30 or 60 at a time or by using multiples of ten:

	432
10 buses	−150
	282
10 buses	−150
	132
4 buses	−60
	72
4 buses	−60
Answer 28 remainder	12
add 1 more bus = 29	

Using 'chunking' to break 432
into numbers associated with 15
432 = 300 + 132
132 = 120 + 12

So 432 = 300 + 120 + 12
20 buses and 8 buses and 1 more

Where there is a context it is important to interpret the result as an answer to the problem rather than give a numerical solution. In the context above the answer '28 remainder 12' will not be appropriate as 29 buses will be needed.

The long-division algorithm is a more condensed way in which to represent the calculation.

$$
\begin{array}{r}
2\ 8 \quad \text{rem } 12 \\
15\overline{)4^{1}3\ 2} \\
3\ 0 \\
\overline{1\ 3\ 2} \\
1\ 2\ 0 \\
\overline{1\ 2}
\end{array}
$$

First 15 is divided into 43 and this will give 2 as the tens part of the answer. The corresponding 30 (tens) are placed under the 43 of the 432. When 30 is subtracted from 43, the 13 gives the number of tens remaining. To this is 'joined' the 2 units to make 13 tens and 2 units, or 132. Now 15 is divided into 132, probably with some pencil and paper jottings e.g. 15, 30, 60, 120 showing 8 × 15 is 120.

This problem could also be solved mentally if the fact that 30 × 15 = 450 is known:

432 = 450 − 18
450 would need 30 buses
18 fewer so 29 buses are needed

For some calculations, initial re-organization into the formal algorithm will be of no help, for example, 'A farm shop sells about 72 eggs each day. How many days will 300 eggs take to sell?'. In this example the traditional long-division algorithm will result in precisely the same problem $300 \div 72$.

$$
\begin{array}{r}
0\ 0\ ? \\
72\overline{)3\ 0^{30}0}
\end{array}
$$

For problems like this it will be necessary to take a different approach or to use a calculator. Approaches based on repeated subtraction will work and the choice of appropriate chunks can make the calculation efficient:

	300
1 day	-72
	228
2 days	-144
	84
1 day	-72
4 days rem	12

	300
4 days	-288
4 days rem	12

A postscript on algorithms

All pupils are expected ultimately to use *efficient* written methods for calculating but the only way such methods can be meaningful is if they are developed progressively to support and extend mental strategies. Recording numbers in a variety of spatial arrangements will be helpful and the identification of an appropriate strategy, whether it is mental, written, or using a calculator, will depend on the problem itself, the numbers involved and the purpose of the calculation. Children will need to develop skills in selecting an appropriate method.

> It is proficiency in [traditional pencil and paper methods] which has in the past been a measure of attainment in mathematics. Such a view can no longer be sustained and, indeed, excessive practice in traditional pencil and paper methods out of context, will act in an inhibiting way to

the overall aim of raising standards in mathematics . . . for most practical purposes, pupils will use mental methods or a calculator to tackle problems involving calculations' (DES, 1989, section E4)

The arguments for continuing to teach written algorithms are usually identified with their conciseness as written records, and the way they encapsulate rules and relationships among numbers in a formal procedure. Their 'elegance' and 'rigour' rather than their utilitarian nature can give them a valued position in mathematics learning provided the purpose in teaching them is made clear to the learners. Plunkett (1979), however, argues that 'the reasons for teaching the standard written algorithm are out of date' and their utilization leads to 'frustration, unhappiness and a deteriorating attitude to mathematics'.

By removing the emphasis on a standard approach it will be possible to focus on the many ways that any problem may be solved, and to focus on the relationships between numbers, and the operations for combining them, that will form the basis for successful problem-solving and more abstract algebraic thinking that will be used in later mathematics.

CHAPTER 7

Decimals, Fractions and Percentages

When children are used to working with numbers by relating them to each other in ways that have been identified in earlier chapters, extensions to fractions, decimals and percentages will reflect familiar patterns of representing numbers and operating with them. Skills have to be learned for these systems of numbers including:

- reading and interpreting the symbols;
- locating the numbers on a number line;
- calculating with these numbers.

Without the appropriate connections it will seem to children that they have totally new systems of symbols and new rules to learn. Children need to learn how to move among the various possible representations in a flexible manner:

> if they (children) know that $\frac{1}{2}$, 0.5 and 50% are all ways of representing the same part of a whole, then the calculations
> $$\frac{1}{2} \times 40$$
> $$40 \times 0.5$$
> $$50\% \text{ of } £40$$
> can be seen as different versions of the same calculation. (QCA, 1999, p. 52)

But each representation brings with it all the conventions for interpreting and operating with the symbols, and the idea that *rational* numbers (that is, any number that can be expressed as a ratio of two numbers) have equivalence representations as fractions, decimals and percentages is far from obvious.

It has been traditional to start with fractions and then extend to equivalent decimals and to percentages. Alternative approaches have been researched and Moss and Case (1999) report a successful teaching experiment beginning with percentages rather than fractions and decimals. Their justification was to 'capitalize on children's pre-existing knowledge' of whole numbers and to postpone 'the problem of having to compare and manipulate ratios'.

Because all percentages have an easy representation as a fraction, for example, 27% is $^{27}/_{100}$, conversion from percentages to fractions is straightforward and children can make conversions 'in a direct and intuitive fashion'. This is not true of the conversion from fractions to percentages as simple fractions such as $\frac{1}{3}$ and $\frac{1}{7}$ do not have easy equivalents as percentages. The decimal equivalents are also straightforward as $^{27}/_{100} = 0.27$. Through this approach, starting with percentages, the children in the study developed 'better global understanding' and 'the sort of confidence, flexibility, and inventiveness. . . . called for . . . in number sense' (Moss and Case, 1999, p. 143).

Starting with percentages

Children's everyday experiences provide contexts in which percentages appear and many will have intuitive ideas of what different numerical values mean. Many appear to have understanding that, for example, 99% means 'almost everything', 50% means 'exactly half' and that 1% means 'very little'. Such intuitive meanings can help guide understanding of the equivalent forms as decimals and fractions, particularly if children work from familiar 'benchmarks' such as the equivalent forms for 50%, 25% and 10%.

Visual imagery for illustrating percentages includes a 100 square with various portions shaded to give the children a sense of 'how many parts out of 100' but another useful image is the number line showing 0% to 100%. This image is often used on computers to show how much of a procedure has been executed and can provide a familiar icon to help connect children's intuitions about proportions to the percentage scale.

Operating with percentages will use the children's experiences with whole number computation, including halving and doubling strategies and may be used to introduce ideas of proportions and relate 10% as 0.1 and 1% as 0.01. Once again, the 'benchmarks' of 0.1 as 10% and 0.01 as 1% provide meanings for the relative size of different decimals that can give children a 'feel' for such numbers.

Establishing the meaning of decimal numbers

The formalization of decimal representation for numbers less than one involves an extension of the place value system to include tenths, hundredths and so on, and social convention can make it difficult for children to interpret the symbolic representation and to locate decimal numbers in relation to each other. The convention of giving large numbers names relating to their size, for example 54 is 'fifty-four' and 540 is 'five hundred and forty', is not extended to decimals and 0.54 is rarely read as 5 tenths and 4 hundredths and is usually read as 'nought point five four' involving language that does not associate the digits with their relative place value.

There is a great temptation for children to 'read' the symbols as whole numbers, for example 0.54 as 'nought point fifty-four' and consequently identify this as a larger number than 0.7. When asked if there is a difference between 4.9 and 4.90 research has shown that many children respond like Frances (age 11) by saying, 'Yes, 4.90 is more' (Brown, 1981b). Complexities also arise because two-digit decimals are commonly used for money and measures with 1.25 read as 'one twenty-five' where the five may also be considered as 'units'.

Multiplying and dividing by ten

Initially the decimal point is introduced to separate the whole part of a number from the fractional part. The idea that multiplying by ten 'shifts' all numbers to the left and dividing by ten 'shifts' all numbers to the right may be explained in terms of column headings (units, tens, hundreds ... extending to the left, and tenths, hundredths ... extending to the right) where the decimal point separates whole numbers from parts of a whole. This idea can cause difficulties not only because of the similarity of the column labels and the complexity of the word constructions, but also because the labels are meaningless until children have some appreciation of the meaning of tenths and hundredths. This is where associating one tenth with 10% and one hundredth with 1% can help children make sense of the relative size of decimals.

Since numbers rarely come with the column labels already in

evidence, it is better to interpret decimal numbers by considering the position of the decimal point and looking at the effect of multiplying and dividing by ten. The idea of multiplying and dividing by ten may be associated with 'shifting the decimal point' and activities involving multiplying and dividing by ten repeatedly using a calculator, will help to establish the pattern of behaviour. Rousham (1999) describes such activities and refers to the 'feedback loop' that involves children in reflecting on the output and learning through the patterns observed. Difficulties can persist into secondary schooling and Hart (1981) found that asking 13-year-old pupils to 'multiply 5.13 by ten' resulted in the responses such as 5.130, obtained by 'adding a zero', and 50.130 which dealt with the two parts of the number (before and after the decimal point) separately.

Flexibility is needed in reading decimals such as 1.25 because the .25 represents 2 tenths and 5 hundredths but at the same time this is 25 hundredths. If children are able to recognize such numbers as 1200 flexibly as 12 hundred as well as 1 thousand and 2 hundreds, this idea with whole numbers can be related to the system of numbers after the decimal point. Whole numbers such as 47 can be written as 47.0 or 47.00 so that moves of the decimal point can again be interpreted in relation to whole numbers.

Operations with decimals

In the same way that number sense for working with whole numbers involves some number relationships that provide 'benchmarks' from which other results may be derived, similar benchmarks need to be established for working with decimals.

Identifying decimals that add to one can establish links with whole number computation, for example by joining the decimals in the top and bottom line that add to a whole number:

0.2	1.75	2.5	0.37	2.8	3.62	54.9	6.3

1.2	0.7	2.25	0.8	23.1	6.5	0.63	1.38

Intuitive ideas cannot be replaced by algorithmic procedures, that is sets of rules for setting out and working through calculations, but a vertical arrangement with the decimal points lined up will provide a calculation method for addition and subtraction that is parallel to the algorithm for whole numbers. Provided pupils have the under-standing to make estimations and check the appropriateness of solutions, this can be the most efficient written method when a calculator is not available.

Multiplication and division with decimals

Experiences with whole numbers can establish meanings for multi-plication and division associated with 'repeated addition', and 'repeated subtraction' or 'sharing'. Discussion in the previous chapter notes that such notions are behind the misconceptions that 'multiplication makes bigger' and 'division makes smaller' (Fisch-bein *et al.*, 1985). When it comes to calculations with decimals, children may struggle to attach a meaning to such calculations as 8 × 0.4 and 8 ÷ 0.4 and when deciding on which operation to use for solving a problem, the wrong operation is often selected. When asked to 'Ring the one which gives the BIGGER answer: 8 × 0.4 or 8 ÷ 0.4', Hart (1981) found that 58% of 13-year-olds circled the first. It is here that associations with the alternative representations of 0.4 as $\frac{4}{10}$ or 40% can help to establish a more meaningful calculation and flexibility in using different representations will add to the 'sense' that children make of such calculations. Where decimal calculations are derived from calculations that are familiar, children will be better able to make sense of their meanings.

'Chains' of calculations can be recorded to show related facts:

$$\boxed{12 \div 4 = 3} \rightarrow \boxed{12 \div 8 = 1.5} \rightarrow \boxed{6 \div 8 = 0.75}$$

$$\boxed{6 \div 1 = 6} \rightarrow \boxed{6 \div 0.5 = 12} \rightarrow \boxed{6 \div 0.25 = 24}$$

$$\downarrow$$

$$\boxed{1.5 \div 0.5 = 3} \leftarrow \boxed{3 \div 0.5 = 6}$$

Introducing fractions

Much of the focus in school work is the identification of fractions as part of a whole or part of a collection. Early experiences with fractions involve practical activities including cutting and sharing with representation that may be in pictures and words before the symbols are introduced. Geometric arrangements of objects, for example pegs on a peg board, will then help children to relate fractions of a shape to a fraction of a collection and begin to use the language that will help them appreciate that the ratio between different numbers can give different representations of the same fraction, for example one half is the same as two quarters.

It is important to develop flexibility in using words and symbols and to identify links with the multiplication facts that children already know. Success with fractions will depend on the appreciation that a fraction represents both a number and a ratio that reflects the procedure for finding this number. The symbol $\frac{3}{4}$ represents a number between $\frac{1}{2}$ and 1, three parts out of four from a whole, and also the result of dividing three by four. It is these latter identifications that enable children to understand that $\frac{6}{8}$, $\frac{15}{20}$ and $\frac{75}{100}$ all represent the *same number*. The latter representation will be crucial for identifying $\frac{3}{4}$ with 0.75 and with 75%. Research suggests that an approach to fractions which identifies each as numbers to be located on a number line, without emphasizing the way of partitioning a whole, will help to establish the equivalence with decimals and percentages.

Locating fractions on the number line

Working initially with fractions with '1' on top (the numerator) their positions on the number line will involve a reversal of the children's normal understanding of relative size and will give a pattern where the distances between fractions (for example, between $\frac{1}{3}$ and $\frac{1}{4}$) are not unit distances as the children might expect (Figure 7.1a).

By keeping the number on the bottom (the denominator) fixed and varying the number on top (the numerator), children can learn to position various fractions and relate their ordering to the counting sequence for whole numbers. Working initially with numbers between 0 and 2, numbers will be introduced as 'top heavy'

Figure 7.1   (a) Distances between ½, ⅓ and ¼ are different.
(b) Equivalent fractions on a number line.

fractions and as 'mixed numbers'. By representing different 'famil-ies' of fractions on the same diagram, ideas of equivalence will be illustrated (Figure 7.1b). It is here that familiarity with multi-plication facts is most crucial so that a fraction can be recognized in many different formats. Extension along the number line will provide opportunities to relate the different representations to multiplication facts where the ratios of numbers can appear in different forms. Some fractions will be easy to link with decimals and percentage representations, such as ½, ¼, ¾, ⅕ or ⅒ and these will provide the 'benchmarks' from which other equivalences can be derived. In using symbols and in calculating, children should be encouraged to use as many interpretations as possible and to link the different representations (Figure 7.2).

Without being aware of it, limitations are imposed on mathemat-ical understanding by conventions that appear to be well established in the classroom and it will take awareness and effort to open children's minds to the wealth of ideas associated with frac-tion representation. Research has shown that 15-year-olds have problems when asked to identify a fraction between ½ and ⅔ and in a study by Hart (1981) only 21% were able to answer correctly.

Mike Askew (2000) identifies one illustration of the way a social convention can restrict the possible mathematics within a situation (Figure 7.3). He suggests that if you ask teachers or primary school pupils what fraction is represented in Figure 7.3 most will say ⅗ (or

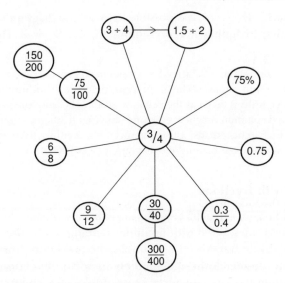

Figure 7.2 A 'web' diagram for ¾.

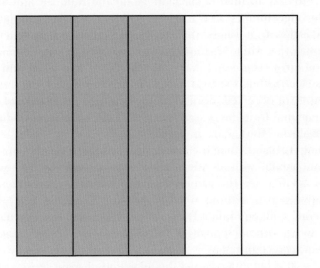

Figure 7.3 A fraction illustration.

$\frac{2}{5}$ or possibly both). However, it is possible to 'read' the diagram in many other ways, including it representing $1\frac{2}{3}$, $2\frac{1}{2}$, $1\frac{1}{2}$ or $\frac{2}{3}$. He suggests that

> the reason it is almost universally read as $\frac{3}{5}$ is not to do with the diagram *per se*, nor to do with pupils' ability to perceive the fraction within the diagram. Three-fifths is taken as the common reading because this is a well established common practice: everyone else from textbook writers to teachers to parents 'reads' the diagram as three-fifths. A social practice is at the heart of reading the diagram. (Askew, 2000)

Calculations with fractions

For many generations, calculations with fractions were practised by following learned rules, often with no understanding of why these rules work. To divide fractions, for example, the procedure 'turn the second one upside down and multiply' is still a mysterious process that cannot be explained by many adults. For children today, understanding is more important as it gives them confidence to think about the problems and to learn the relationships that will extend beyond arithmetic calculations and provide the foundations for algebra. Research has shown that ideas of adding and subtracting have presented difficulties throughout schooling and Hart found that when 12–15-year-olds were asked to add $\frac{1}{3}$ and $\frac{1}{4}$ a common error (made by 1 in 5 of the children) was to respond $\frac{2}{7}$, the result of adding the tops and adding the bottoms. She notes that this error occurred more when the problem was presented in computational form (as a sum) than when it was presented in a word problem (Hart, 1981, p. 75).

Adding and subtracting fractions is only possible if they belong to the same 'family' with identical *denominators* (that is the numbers on the bottom are the same). To add $\frac{1}{2}$ and $\frac{2}{5}$, for example, alternative representations need to be found and this is where experiences with equivalent fractions are important. Even then, to add $\frac{5}{10}$ and $\frac{4}{10}$ without applying a 'rule' will only be possible if these numbers are recognized as '5 tenths' and '4 tenths', together giving '9 tenths'. It is better to discuss the meanings of these representations rather than introduce rules, such as 'add the tops', because children who understand will remember better the procedures and be able to transfer similar working to other situations. As the final step in the procedure, the resulting fraction, in this case $\frac{9}{10}$, must be adjusted, if necessary, to its *lowest* form with no common factors in the *numerator* (top) and *denominator* (bottom). It must be appreciated that children's knowledge of equivalent fractions will depend on their knowledge of multiplication facts and their ability to interpret flexibly the symbols they are working with.

Steps in the procedure for subtracting $\frac{1}{5}$ from $\frac{3}{4}$:

1. Find a 'family' that involves both fifths and quarters. This can be achieved by looking for a multiple of 5 that is also a multiple of 4.

2. Having found 20 as the smallest common multiple, change $\frac{1}{5}$ and $\frac{3}{4}$ to equivalent fractions in the family of 'twentieths'. By multiplying top and bottom of $\frac{1}{5}$ by 4, the ratio is preserved and the equivalent fraction $\frac{4}{20}$ is obtained. Similarly, multiplying the top and bottom of $\frac{3}{4}$ by 5 gives the equivalent fraction $\frac{15}{20}$.

3. Subtract '4 twentieths' from '15 twentieths', leaving '11 twentieths'.

4. Check that 11 and 20 have no common factors so that $\frac{11}{20}$ is in its lowest form.

If the resulting fraction was not in its lowest terms, for example $\frac{12}{20}$, an equivalent fraction is found by dividing top and bottom by the same factors, in this case 4, reducing the fraction to $\frac{3}{5}$.

Multiplying fractions

The conversion to fractions in the same family is not necessary for multiplication and division but, starting with multiplication by a whole number, there are many stages in coming to *understand* the processes involved. At each stage it will be necessary to 'read' the symbols flexibly and discussion can be more helpful than working only with the written symbols on a page. Using the commutative rule for multiplication means that calculations such as $\frac{3}{4} \times 6$ and $6 \times \frac{3}{4}$ may both be interpreted as '6 lots of $\frac{3}{4}$' and pictorial representation may be helpful in making this a meaningful calculation. Once again, interpreting $\frac{3}{4}$ as '3 quarters' will also be helpful in calculating the total of '18 quarters', and this may be identified with '4 wholes and 2 quarters'. The alternative interpretation of $\frac{3}{4} \times 6$ and $6 \times \frac{3}{4}$ involves the calculation of 'three quarters of 6'. This is not easy to reconcile with the symbol '×' unless the phrase 'lots of' is adjusted to '$\frac{3}{4}$ of' and this is not immediately clear. The representations of '$\frac{3}{4}$ of 6' and '6 lots of $\frac{3}{4}$' will determine the same result (Figure 7.4).

The same result will also be obtained by 'multiplying 6 by 3 and dividing by 4' which is an alternative way of 'multiplying by $\frac{3}{4}$'. All of these interpretations give different ways to calculate the result and may be related to different illustrations.

The purpose in manipulating fractions in this way is not so much for usefulness in problem solving but more to explore the underlying relationships that exist within such calculations. When pupils meet algebra in secondary schools, all of these different interpretations will be identified with rules for manipulating abstract expressions, but in primary school the actual quantities are helpful in identifying the patterns of behaviour as fractions are multiplied.

The next stage in multiplication involves fractions for both numbers and a meaning must be sought for interpreting calculations such as '$\frac{2}{3} \times \frac{1}{5}$'. The equivalent operations 'multiplying by one fifth', 'finding one fifth of...' and 'dividing by 5' all lead to the result '$\frac{2}{15}$' which can be illustrated diagrammatically. It is also possible to apply the 'rectangle method' for multiplying starting with the representation of $\frac{2}{3}$ and $\frac{1}{5}$ of a shape. Once again the resultant $\frac{2}{15}$ will be the area shaded. The 'rule' that results is to 'multiply the tops' and to 'multiply the bottoms' and this may be established by considering the results of many examples involving different numbers. Working with the 'rule' and checking with an illustration will help to show that it will not always be necessary to consider the meaning, and calculations can be undertaken with the confidence that they can be explained if necessary.

Dividing fractions

As with multiplication, division with fractions starts by giving meaning to division involving one of the numbers as a whole number. Since the commutative rule does not apply to division, the expressions '$4 \div \frac{1}{2}$' and '$\frac{1}{2} \div 4$' will need to be interpreted separately. As suggested in Chapter 4, the expressions most easily understood will be different for each of these expressions with 'How many halves in

Figure 7.4 '6 lots of $\frac{3}{4}$' and '$\frac{3}{4}$ of 6'.

4?' and '$\frac{1}{2}$ divided into 4 (parts)' providing imagery that will enable each to be tackled by a different procedure. This ability to interpret a division expression in the most convenient way is at the heart of successful calculating where a whole number is involved. Some children will be uncomfortable with the idea that a division calculation can result in a number that is larger than either of the starting numbers, as 'division makes smaller' can be an intuitive idea associated with division as sharing (Fischbein *et al.* 1985) or as repeated subtraction. For this reason, some time may be needed to give meanings to division expressions involving fractions so that children themselves can be confident that they can find a meaning for each example. Using a calculator to look at patterns, for example dividing several numbers by $\frac{1}{2}$ or $\frac{1}{4}$, can be helpful where the equivalent formats as the decimals 0.5 and 0.25 are understood.

In order to explain division involving two fractions, the idea of ratios can be used. First it is helpful to know about 'multiplicative inverses' as fraction numbers that 'undo' each other in multiplication. If the fraction $\frac{3}{4}$ is multiplied by $\frac{4}{3}$ the result will be $\frac{12}{12}$ or simply 1. The fractions $\frac{3}{4}$ and $\frac{4}{3}$ are called 'multiplicative inverses' as they multiply together to give the number 1. Similarly, any fraction can be 'undone' in this way using a fraction number with the top and bottom inverted, that is, the fraction 'turned upside down'.

Now consider the calculation $\frac{2}{3} \div \frac{3}{5}$:

Step 1: rewrite this expression as a ratio, $\dfrac{\frac{2}{3}}{\frac{3}{5}}$.

Step 2: change this ratio into an equivalent fraction by multiplying the top and bottom by the same number. The number is chosen so that the bottom number becomes 1. That is, multiply the top and bottom by $\frac{5}{3}$, the multiplicative inverse of $\frac{3}{5}$.

Step 3: now the calculation has become $\dfrac{\frac{2}{3} \times \frac{5}{3}}{\frac{3}{5} \times \frac{5}{3}}$ and this is equivalent to $\frac{2}{3} \times \frac{5}{3}$.

This shows how division is achieved by 'turning the second fraction upside down and multiplying' but gives an explanation of why this works rather than offering it as a mysterious rule to be remembered.

Working with fractions or decimals

Since the systems of measurements today are predominantly metric, fractions appear less frequently in everyday situations than in the past and some children may prefer to work by changing fractions to equivalent decimals. This will be necessary if the calculation is to be undertaken with a calculator as few calculators work with numbers in fraction format. In the calculation, $\frac{3}{4} - \frac{1}{5}$ (p. 119), children may be happier with the alternative representation as 0.75 − 0.2 since both fractions may be familiar as decimals. This calculation will then depend on subtracting '2 tenths' from '7 tenths' and the result 0.55 may be changed back to the fraction for $\frac{55}{100}$ or $\frac{11}{20}$ if required.

Using technology

Division can soon present difficulties where numbers do not divide exactly and 'remainders' can be interpreted as fractions or as decimals. This occurs frequently in problems set in a real world context. Working with calculators will enable children to focus on selecting an appropriate operation to solve the problem and interpreting the solution. This may also provide an opportunity to help them understand the relationship between multiplication and division by using the inverse operation to check calculations. Work with related division calculations can generate interesting solutions. The problems 'How many biscuits each if 26 biscuits are shared amongst 5 children or 4 children or 3 children?' lead to

Table 7.1 Different ways to record and check solutions.

division problem	mental solution	calculator solution	multiplication
$26 \div 5$	5 with 1 left or 5 and one fifth	$26 \div 5 = 5.2$	$5 \times 5.2 = 26$
$26 \div 4$	6 with 2 left or $2\frac{1}{2}$	$26 \div 4 = 6.5$	$4 \times 6.5 = 26$
$26 \div 3$	8 with 2 left or 8 and 2 thirds	$26 \div 3$ $= 8.6666666$	3×8.6666666 $= 25.999999$

the very different results that can be discussed and compared (Table 7.1).

Division by 4 and 5 will be easier to understand as the decimal fractions involved may be familiar. Division by 3 can introduce a long 'tail' of decimal numbers that may be related back to the original problem when looking for an explanation. Such difficulties should not be avoided but taken as a focus for discussion to raise children's awareness that such complexities arise.

Using spreadsheets to explore ratios set up between column entries can be a powerful way to develop experiences of multiplicative relationships that do not rely on repeated addition. This also reinforces the idea of the *ratio* between numbers in the different columns and this will be a most useful way of representing multiplication and division relationships in secondary schooling.

CHAPTER 8

Teaching Approaches

The chapters of this book have aimed to show how the foundations of number sense can be seen in the connections that show how numbers relate to each other within a logical structure and how new facts can be linked to those that are already known. This chapter will discuss the teaching approaches that are most appropriate in developing children's number sense and will make references to some pertinent research studies.

Working with numbers in context

The traditional sequence of school activities, from easy numbers and their representation to complex numbers and calculations, does not take account of the way children learn. Just as language is developed by exposing children to a rich environment of words used in appropriate contexts, so number sense begins to develop when they are presented with opportunities to talk about numbers wherever they occur. Learning takes place whenever children reflect on what they are seeing and hearing, and involvement in 'number conversations' can begin from the earliest age. Personal experiences (for example, four sweets — and eat one makes three!, the number 35 bus, a second chance, 20p for the hair dryer at the swimming pool) are starting points that should not be ignored. If children are exposed to numbers in this way, numbers will have meaning within a real context and children will use them confidently, identifying mathematics as a powerful tool for making sense of the world.

Numbers need to be presented in a realistic setting in order to make sense to young children. However, they can and should also be presented orally, as linguistic entities in their own right. To be able to count 'one hundred, two hundred, three hundred...' does not indicate that these numbers are understood but the fascination of 'inventing' such large numbers reinforces a pattern that is generalizable and fundamental in the number system. As the chapters of this book have shown, counting is a key skill for understanding numbers. Aubrey (1997) reports that on entry to schooling 'the children with highest rote counting scores tended to have consistently high scores across [a range of] number tasks'. These tasks include counting backwards and simple number operations. She notes that 'teachers' intuitive knowledge about children and teaching may *not* be well connected' (original italics) to what children are already capable of and proposes that teaching needs to focus on 'fine-grain analysis of the way teaching and learning interact' in order to develop most effectively children's existing number sense (Aubrey, 1997, p. 29). Research evidence also suggests that very young children are capable of handling larger numbers in more complex ways than teachers have conventionally believed or assumed (Munn, 1994; Merttens, 1996; Thompson, 1997).

Whitebread (1999) advocates the approach to teaching which is referred to as 'emergent mathematics' in parallel with ideas of 'emergent writing'. It is based on the theory that children need to develop their understanding of numbers by playing with them and using them for their own purposes. In such an approach, children are invited to talk about their mathematical ideas with other children and with the teacher. They are encouraged to focus on mathematical processes and represent them in a way that makes sense to them, so becoming aware of their own and other people's thinking. By presenting real problems to be tackled in a meaningful context it will not always be appropriate to limit the numbers involved but this will give a better impression of the ways that mathematics is relevant to their lives than abstract activities from schemes or texts. By involving children in the sorts of activities that reflect everyday use of numbers they become aware of *how* numbers are used and also *why* they are used. As a result they develop the motivation to master for themselves the many skills and connections that explain number work.

In an 'emergent' approach children are encouraged 'to make their own representations of mathematical problems, processes and procedures before they are introduced to the conventional symbols', because the emphasis is on developing confidence in their own thinking (Whitebread, 1999, p. 31). Although children may well notice conventional symbols from an early age (for example, '+' and '−' on video controls), they need to take the initiative in using them when *they* think these are appropriate to express *their* ideas and findings. Children's own representations give clues about how they are working things out and this 'enables teachers to assess and build on children's thinking and prevents the inappropriate imposition of images on their thinking' (Gifford, 1997, p. 86). Traditional sums presented as written tasks can limit children's experiences where symbols such as '+', '−' and '=' are given narrow meanings and this can lead to inflexible use of such symbols. By sharing their own ideas about the way calculations can be recorded, under the guidance of a teacher, young children can be exposed to a great many ways of writing mathematics while retaining ownership of their personal ideas.

Meta-cognitive awareness and control are also identified as important features of emergent mathematics; not only do children develop strategies, they also develop the ability to use them appropriately (Whitebread, 1999). This ability to consider different possible procedures is called 'meta-cognitive' since the *procedures* occur at the cognitive 'level' while *reflecting on them* occurs at a higher 'level' of awareness. Knowing that adding 19 is best achieved by adding 20 and subtracting 1, while adding 12 is best achieved by adding 10 and then 2 more, are examples where meta-cognitive awareness will result in different procedures for adding according to the number involved. Although children may learn some standard procedures, using number sense involves departure from these methods where the numbers warrant a different approach.

Building on what children know when they start school

Some children have difficulty relating the number work they encounter on entering school, with the use of numbers they have experienced outside school. Aubrey (1997) discusses the 'gap between children's own informal, invented number knowledge and the formal requirements of the reception class curriculum'. She reports that in a research project attempting to shed light on typical early years practice it became clear that this 'does not match the range and diversity of knowledge, skills and strategies in a variety of number, counting and arithmetic tasks for children entering school'. In the first, and even more in the second, year of schooling, schemes and worksheets were thought 'to offer a framework for planning the introduction of sorting, matching and ordering numbers' that did not reflect the stage of children's understanding or take account of children's informal knowledge. Inappropriate emphasis was placed on 'practical colour, pattern and shape recognition, matching, sorting and ordering of shape, comparison and ordering of quantity, counting and recording and comparison of sets' (Aubrey, 1997, p. 23). 'Children did not appear to relate their in-school activities with structured materials to their out-of-school, context specific problem solving.' Findings of the research suggest that teachers' intuitive knowledge about what activities are appropriate for consolidating or extending the understanding of their pupils can be better informed by analysis of the children's existing knowledge. Research shows that 'pupils learn more when their teachers know their attainment and can act on this information' (Askew and Wiliam, 1995, p. 20).

To help children transfer their informal knowledge of numbers to practical applications of this knowledge in the classroom, activities can be devised to reflect situations outside school where numbers have been seen and used. Role play areas in the classroom such as a café or pet shop present opportunities for children to recognize numerals and use the language of numbers. Activities such as making price tags, or organizing money in a cash box, give realistic purposes for number work and can generate discussion through which formal language and symbols may be introduced. Working together, beginning to record and to share ideas, will be an important way to develop skills in mathematical thinking and to establish methods for communicating this thinking through words, pictures and symbols.

Diversity in children's mastery of number facts can make it difficult for the teacher as the number work of individual children will progress at different rates that need to be monitored but cannot be predicted. Until they enter school, learning has taken place within the child's family and the wider community, through involvement in talking and thinking about issues that have arisen. Much of the children's learning will continue to be developed outside the classroom and a partnership between school and home will be needed to establish common goals and learning objectives that are shared with parents and carers (Merttens and Vass, 1993).

Teachers as listeners

A key characteristic of early learning in the home is the opportunity for conversations in which the child, as the learner, often takes the initiative in asking the questions. Although this is not always possible in the classroom, an environment where children are encouraged to express their thinking and ask questions as well as answer them will encourage independent approaches to problem solving. Children will need opportunities to talk about their own strategies and to discuss those used by others. Whether working orally or with written problems, it is important to listen to the explanations of individual children in order to ascertain their grasp of particular relationships and their ability to apply number sense rather than doggedly replicating a learned procedure. The following examples illustrate responses that show a range of strategies for addition that were given by a child to explain the answers to mental calculations:

$[5 + 2 = 7]$ '5, 6, 7'
$[2 + 2 = 4]$ 'because I know 2 and 2'
$[3 + 4 = 7]$ '3 and 3 is 6 and one more is 7'
$[5 + 4 = 9]$ 'because it is one less than 10'

Each of these explanations refers to a different procedure for solving the addition problems and the variations show the way in which children can develop flexibility by selecting the most appropriate procedure for each problem. As they meet problems in a variety of contexts children will often respond more readily if the numerical calculations have some explicit meaning for themselves (for example, 'You are 5 years old and Stephen is 7. How much older is Stephen?'). Although the ultimate aim is for instant recall of basic number facts, such as the pairs that make 10 and other combinations such as 25 and 25, the strategies children develop on the way to knowing these facts will form the basis for calculation with larger numbers. Research results show that 'knowing by heart' and 'figuring out' support each other in children's learning about numbers (Askew and Wiliam, 1995, p. 8).

In developing mental calculating strategies, teachers need to pay careful attention to children's actions and words so that they may appreciate the subtle differences that exist. This will help them to identify those who have achieved efficiency in their approaches and those who are persisting with more naïve and inefficient strategies. Children can learn to choose the calculation method with fewest steps (for example 11 − 3 would be calculated by counting back, while 11 − 8 would be calculated by counting on) but presenting appropriate examples, can help to clarify the benefits of different approaches. More extreme examples (such as 34 − 5 and 34 − 28) can be introduced to stimulate discussion about effective approaches.

There can be difficulties for teachers where much of the calculating is done orally and little written recording takes place. Emma Brown (1997) reports that, although she encourages mental mathematics in her classroom, she admits finding it problematic with respect to 'assessment and some kind of monitoring of progress'. Where there are no written records of the mental strategy children are using, discussion becomes even more important as a way to monitor the children's thinking. Recording some of the ideas will be necessary for clear communication and this can be the focus of follow-up work, rather than the driving force in the calculating process. There may be some scepticism from the public at large in placing the emphasis on mental mathematics rather than written recording, as there often is whenever traditions are challenged. Teachers will need to use the available research and survey evidence to help persuade parents that delaying written calculating methods is educationally sound.

Teaching number work as a social activity

Talking is a powerful tool as children continue to learn by listening and joining in conversations, using their logic and developing their language to match different situations. Mathematical learning will be dependent on the children being ready to reflect on the results of their thinking and make the transition to discuss results themselves. The classroom practice of children sharing in the learning process is sometimes referred to as *collective reflection* and identified with the *socio-norms* of the classroom through which children learn what is universally accepted and acceptable (Cobb *et al.*, 1997).

Researchers have found it helpful to use the notion of *reflectiv.* *discourse* to describe the classroom talk through which mathematical activity itself is objectified and becomes an explicit topic of conversation. The teacher's role is to guide and initiate shifts in this discourse so that what was previously done in action becomes an explicit topic of conversation.

Cobb *et al.* (1997) use an anecdote to explain the development of mathematical thinking that is possible under teacher guidance. Starting with visual images of five monkeys in two trees, the children proceed, working mentally or with their fingers as 'perceptual substitutes', and propose different ways the monkeys could be distributed:

Anna: I think that three could be in the little tree and two could be in the big tree.

Teacher: OK, three could be in the little tree and two could be in the big tree [writes 3/2 between the trees]. So, still 3 and 2 but they are in different trees this time; three in the little one and two in the big one. Linda you have another way?

Linda: Five could be in the big one.

Teacher: OK, five could be in the big one [writes 5] and then how many would be in the little one?

Linda: Zero.

Here the teacher gives a commentary from the perspective of one who could judge which aspects of the children's activity might be mathematically significant within what the researchers refer to as *mathematizing discourse*. The teacher later asks:

> 'Is there a way that we could be sure and know we've gotten all the ways?'

Now the results of the activity become explicit objects of the discussion that can be related to each other. The discourse shifts from generating the possible ways, to operating on the results of that generative activity − this could lead to a systematic ordering of results and strategies for testing if the list is complete. Cobb *et al.*

'It is this feature of the episode that leads us to classify
ıple of *reflective* discourse' and conclude that 'children's
n in this type of discourse *constitutes conditions for the
possibility of mathematical learning*' (Cobb *et al.*, 1997, p. 264).

Identifying and working with misconceptions

Although it is tempting in a class discussion to invite children whose
responses are correct to talk about the way they tackled a solution,
it is important to create an environment that accepts every child's
thinking as equally valid. Asking a child 'How did you arrive at that
answer?' when the answer is incorrect, will sometimes lead to
individuals reviewing their procedures and correcting themselves,
but may also lead to opportunities for other children to help put
right any erroneous ideas. Rather than 'spreading' misconceptions
through sharing them, children will learn to reason about their
strategies and follow the reasoning of others, thus developing
important skills in communication of mathematical thinking.
Askew and Wiliam (1995) cite research evidence that supports the
idea that learning is more effective when common misconceptions
are addressed, exposed and discussed in teaching. 'We have to
accept that pupils will make some generalizations that are not
correct and many of these misconceptions remain hidden unless
the teacher makes specific efforts to uncover them' (Askew and
Wiliam, 1995, p. 12).

Many children will have misconceptions and make wrong generalizations at some stage in their mathematical learning. In an
effort to find more efficient ways of working, able pupils will
sometimes try to apply rules that they know in new situations or
make wrong generalizations. In the counting sequence, twenty-
nine followed by twenty-ten, for example, shows a child's sound
strategy that does not apply in this particular situation. Verbalizing
such thinking will not only help the child involved but also all
children can benefit by 'seeing' how other people are thinking
about numbers.

Watching and listening to children is important for detecting
errors and misconceptions. In the example '11 − 3', for example,
the number eleven is sometimes included within the three to be

132

counted (11, 10, 9) and the wrong answer '9' is given. It is important to identify such misconceptions early and work again with concrete materials or imagined contexts ('If I start with 11 buttons in a row and cover up 3, how many will I still see?'). Encouraging children to use their fingers and count out loud will give opportunities to assess their strategies. In his 'alternative approach' to the number curriculum, Thompson proposes that one of the actions to be incorporated into classroom teaching is 'to legitimate and encourage the use of fingers and counting procedures particularly for simple addition and subtraction' (Thompson, 1997, p. 157).

Characterizing effective teaching approaches

The previous section suggests that classroom talk is an essential element of effective teaching and this section will go on to look at a study that has attempted to characterize the most effective teaching approaches for mathematics in primary school. In a study of effective numeracy teaching, Askew *et al.* (1997) use the term '*connectionist*' to describe approaches where emphasis is given to the links between different ideas in mathematics and to encouraging pupils to draw on their mathematical understanding to develop their own strategies in problem solving. By gathering evidence from a sample of 90 teachers the researchers found out what teachers believed, knew, understood and did. The study gained data on resulting outcomes in terms of pupil learning gains for over 2000 pupils. In this study the researchers found that highly effective teachers believe that pupils develop strategies and networks of ideas by being challenged to think, through explaining, listening and problem solving, and use teaching approaches that build on pupils' own mental strategies with teacher intervention to make these more efficient. This teacher intervention appears to be crucial in developing children's ideas in a progressive way.

A different category of teaching approach identified in this study is that of the '*discovery*' orientated teacher who tended to treat all methods of calculation as equally acceptable. This approach focused on encouraging pupils' creation of their own methods and was based on building their confidence and ability in practical methods. These teachers' primary belief was that 'becoming numerate is an individual activity derived from actions on objects'. Such teachers also believe that pupils' own strategies are the most important and that pupil misunderstandings are 'the result of pupils not being "ready" to learn the ideas'. This contrasts with the connectionist orientation view that 'pupils' misunderstandings need to be recognized, made explicit and worked on' with pupils being 'challenged and struggling to overcome difficulties'.

A third category was identified as those teachers who believed in the importance of their pupils acquiring a collection of procedures or routines, particularly in regard to pencil and paper methods. These were characterized as having a *'transmission'* orientation encompassing the view that teaching is most effective through verbal explanations of routines and results in the use of 'track laying' − the use of pencil and paper methods with styles of recording in advance of when they may be appropriate. As an example of this 'track laying', in traditional texts pupils may be introduced to the 'bus shelter' notation for division (e.g. $4\overline{)36}$) at a stage when the problem may be solved by recall. Encouragement is given to use this written algorithmic method which sets out the problems in vertical format and places emphasis on the arrangement where the answer '9 is placed above the 6' (Nuffield 4 *Teacher's Handbook*, 1981). The written recording does not facilitate the calculation but prepares the format that may be used for later, more complex, calculations. Where this is not clear to the children, confusion may arise about the methods they should use to solve the calculation itself.

In this research study, the 'transmission teachers', who gave priority to pupils acquiring a collection of standard arithmetical methods over establishing understanding and connections, produced lower numeracy gains when the children were tested towards the beginning and again towards the end of a school year. Lower numeracy gains were also associated with the 'discovery' approach which gave priority to the use of practical equipment, and delayed the introduction of more abstract ideas 'until [the teacher] felt a child was ready for them'. In the most successful 'connectionist' approach, teachers believed that *being numerate* requires having a rich network of connections between different mathematical ideas and being able to select and use a range strategies (Askew *et al.*, 1997, p. 31).

Teaching mental strategies

Although there has been a long tradition in *mental recall* and children have, for generations, been required to commit to memory a variety of mathematical facts and formulae, early introduction of standard written algorithms has meant that *mental strategies* have not been explicitly taught in the classroom. The progressive development reflected in most schemes and texts has involved stages towards the standard methods to be reproduced and practised in written exercises. In teaching these standard written approaches the expectation has been that children will have an efficient procedure for calculating that they can apply to any number problem. The reality has been that the curtailed written record of a procedure based on manipulating digits, rather than a holistic approach to the numbers involved, has made it difficult (or impossible) to understand, and arithmetic for many children has in the past been reduced to the application of rules. Researchers have shown that the gap between a child's way of thinking about a problem and the formal procedure of an algorithm has presented difficulties that could be avoided with a more progressive approach to gaining efficiency, and more flexibility through written presentation based on mental strategies (Thompson, 1997; Anghileri, 1998 and 1999b).

The teaching of mental calculations has for some time been the focus of research in the Netherlands and van den Heuvel-Panhuizen (2000) identifies ways in which the Dutch curriculum has been developed to support mental strategies. It is the Realistic Mathematics Education (RME) approach to first engage with the children's informal strategies, elaborating on them later, and move towards more formal standard procedures. This is considered to be a much better learning activity than the other way around. Rather than beginning with certain abstractions or definitions to be applied later, teaching starts with rich contexts demanding mathematical organization or, in other words, 'contexts that can be mathematized'. Structured materials such as a 100 bead string and an empty number line are introduced systematically to support mental methods and then written calculations are built progressively from the children's intuitive approaches.

Research has shown the effectiveness of such practices in the

Netherlands compared with more traditional teaching in the UK (Anghileri, 1998, 2000). A characterization of different teaching approaches in the Netherlands and the UK, identifies the benefits of written methods that are more compatible with the sense that children make of different problems (Beishuizen and Anghileri, 1998). 'It is true that, in the beginning, non-standard methods can be time consuming; but if the learners are allowed to develop them further, they become curtailed and more efficient' (Beishuizen, 1997). Where similar teaching approaches have been implemented in the UK, there have been reports on the positive responses that teachers have made to the change of focus from written to mental strategies. Keith Holloway (1997) describes the findings of a group of primary teachers who explored the issues surrounding mental strategies in school. These teachers found that written versions of children's mental strategies show little similarity to standard algorithms and that they are based on different understanding of number. Positive responses were observed amongst the children to mental mathematics, with a rise in self-esteem of a number of individuals. Debates spontaneously occurred where children tried to help others understand their ways of doing things, and as they discussed which ways were more efficient. Instead of removing difficulties, teachers were more likely to pose problems that address directly misconceptions and to encourage children to think divergently with open questions. Teachers reported that 'children have felt freer to express themselves in a confident and accurate way because the format has not been questioning'.

Using calculators to motivate and empower children

In addition to research projects such as those discussed above, there has been a notable curriculum development project in the UK that has influenced ways to develop children's confidence and initiative in working with numbers. The PrIME (Primary Initiatives in Mathematics Education) project (Shuard *et al.*, 1991), with its integrated CAN (Calculator Aware Number) project has had widespread influence on teachers, and the impact of these projects has been recognized around the world. In the innovative approaches introduced in these projects, it was the fundamental policy that no algorithms were taught but that children were encouraged to devise, and to share, their own ways of calculating with a strong emphasis on mental calculations. Teachers did not spend time showing, or trying to show children how to do calculations, but devised tasks that were rich in numerical connections. The emphasis was on creativity as children gained confidence in their own ideas and even began to devise their own mathematical tasks, and this very much involved pattern spotting.

Likening it to the 'creativity and independence more usually experienced in an art class', Rousham (1999) reports the 'enjoyment and changed attitude' to mathematics as children in the project schools wanted to 'do maths for the pleasure of exploring numbers'. The removal of standard procedures for calculating enabled children to try out their own ideas, while correct calculations on the calculator formed the basis for identifying patterns and developing awareness of relationships among numbers and between operations. In his discussion of calculators as a cognitive learning tool in the classroom, Rousham refers to the way 6- and 7-year-olds tackled missing number problems such as $\Delta + \square = 28$. He uses the term 'feedback loop' for the dialogue of question and response that children can have with a calculator. He suggests that the machine not only answers silently and reliably every question, but gives a 'fresh and unasked-for piece of information' that can guide further questioning. This environment may be helpful in preventing children from developing misconceptions. The feedback loop goes beyond a 'trial and improve' method because children become interested in the transient displays in a long calculation and Rousham (1999) reports children sitting and thinking about what is displayed in a manner that is not typical of adults.

Rousham does, however, warn that 'children need real access over some considerable time to become sufficiently familiar and confident with them to cross that "threshold" of familiarity which allows them to use the calculator's power for the kind of high order exploration of tasks' that he noticed during the CAN project.

There was little in the way of formal research evaluation at the time of the PrIME and CAN projects but many anecdotal reports exist that report the effectiveness of the innovative teaching approaches. Subsequent research studies in schools involved with the project have been undertaken. In an evaluation involving 'post-

CAN' schools (that were previously involved with the project) Ruthven (1998) reports that pupils 'were encouraged to develop informal methods of calculation, and to use calculators to explore number and execute demanding computations'. He noted that investigative and problem-solving activities formed an important part of the curriculum and it was here that calculators were most likely to be used. When compared with pupils in schools where calculators were less readily available and 'the sense was more of working towards written methods', he reports that 'while there was acknowledgement of pupils' informal strategies in the non-project schools, there was less emphasis on developing and refining them, and more on adopting approved written methods, predominantly standard column methods'.

In the project schools, pupils had been 'explicitly taught mental methods based on "smashing up" or "breaking down" numbers' and were 'expected to behave responsibly in regulating their use of calculators to complement their mental methods'. In contrast, in the non-project schools, 'daily experience of "quickfire calculation" had offered pupils a model of mental calculation as something to be done quickly or abandoned'. Calculator use provided opportunities for reflection on the output in, what Ruthven termed, an *observe–predict–surpass* or in a *diagnose–explain–reinforce* sequence. Rather than inhibiting pupils' ability to work with mental calculations, Ruthven found that, when tested on standard calculations, the pupils from a 'calculator-aware' environment were more inclined to use mental computation than written column methods or multiple use of a calculator, and were 'less prone to fall back on the use of written or calculator methods'. Additionally, in his conclusions he notes that effective use of the calculator enables pupils to tackle problems which call for computation 'beyond their current capabilities'. Rather than reducing mathematical understanding, attention is turned to the underlying mathematical ideas associated with a calculation (Ruthven, 2000).

Towards a new generation of mathematical thinkers

Whether children are making their own sense of problems or simply trying to reproduce taught procedures will become evident in their approaches to problem solving. When children have con-

A farm shop sells about 72 eggs each day. How many days will 300 eggs take to sell?

$$
\begin{array}{r}
300 \\
-\ 144 \quad \text{(2 days)} \\
\hline
156 \\
-\ 144 \quad \text{(2 days)} \\
\hline
12
\end{array}
$$

So it will take 4 days and a bit so probably about 11:00 on the 5th day.

Figure 8.1 Number sense in problem solving.

fidence in tackling problems they may go beyond minimal requirements in calculating to produce an enhanced solution as in Figure 8.1.

This solution shows a real *feel* for numbers that typifies what can be achieved when teaching is focused on developing children's *number sense*.

When arithmetic is taught as a logical structure of connected processes and results, rather than a sequence of standard procedures, children will learn that there is flexibility and choice in solving problems. As a result, they will develop *ownership* in making decisions and deriving meanings from their actions. It is this ownership that will help them to develop the confidence in their thinking and an *inclination* to work with numbers. If teaching approaches change so that children learn *connections* then the outcome could be a new generation of mathematical thinkers who will be autonomous learners driven on by their fascination with numbers.

References

Anghileri, J. (1995) 'Children's finger methods for multiplication'. *Mathematics in School,* **24** (1).

Anghileri, J. (1997) 'Uses of counting in multiplication and division', in I. Thompson (ed.) *Teaching and Learning Early Number.* Buckingham: Open University Press.

Anghileri, J. (1998) 'A discussion of different approaches to arithmetic teaching', in A. Olivier and K. Newstead (eds) *Proceedings of the Twenty-second International Conference for the Psychology of Mathematics Education, Vol. 2,* pp. 2–17.

Anghileri, J. (1999a) *Children's Mathematical Thinking in the Primary Years* (2nd edn). London: Cassell.

Anghileri, J. (1999b) 'A comparison of English and Dutch year 5 pupils: calculation strategies for division'. *Proceedings of the British Congress on Mathematics Education.* University of Northampton.

Anghileri, J. (2000) *Principles and Practices in Arithmetic Teaching.* Buckingham: Open University Press.

Anghileri, J. and Beishuizen, M. (1998) 'Counting, chunking and the division algorithm'. *Mathematics in School,* **27**(1).

Askew, M. (2000) 'What does it mean to learn? What is effective teaching?', in J. Anghileri (ed.) *Principles and Practices in Arithmetic Teaching.* Buckingham: Open University Press.

Askew, M. and Wiliam, D. (1995) *Recent Research in Mathematics Education 5–16.* London: HMSO.

Askew, M., Brown, M., Rhodes, V., Wiliam, D. and Johnson, D. (1997) *Effective Teachers of Numeracy: Report of a Study Carried Out for the Teacher Training Agency.* London: King's College, University of London.

Aubrey, C. (1997) 'Children's early learning of number in school and out', in I. Thompson (ed.) *Teaching and Learning Early Number.* Buckingham: Open University Press.

AEC (Australian Education Council) (1991) *A National Statement on Mathematics for Australian Schools.* Carlton, Victoria: Curriculum Corporation.

Beishuizen, M. (1995) 'New research into mental arithmetic strategies with two-digit numbers up to 100.' *European Conference on Educational Research, University of Bath, September 1995.*

Beishuizen M. (1997) 'Mental arithmetic: mental recall or mental strategies?'. *Mathematics Teaching*, **160**, 16–19.

Beishuizen, M. (1999) 'The empty number line as a new model', in I. Thompson (ed.) *Issues in Teaching Numeracy in Primary Schools*. Buckingham: Open University Press.

Beishuizen, M. and Anghileri, J. (1998) 'Which mental strategies in the early number curriculum? A comparison of British ideas and Dutch views'. *British Education Research Journal*, **25** (5).

Brown E. (1997) 'Effective exercise in the mathematics classroom'. *Mathematics Teaching*, **160**, 12–15.

Brown, J. and Van Lehn, K. (1982) 'Towards a generative theory of bugs', in Carpenter, T. *et al.* (eds) *Addition and Subtraction: a Cognitive Perspective*. Hillsdale, NJ: Lawrence Erlbaum.

Brown, M. (1981a) 'Number operations', in K. Hart (ed.) *Children's Understanding of Mathematics: 11–16*. London: Murray.

Brown, M. (1981b) 'Place value and decimals', in K. Hart (ed.) *Children's Understanding of Mathematics 11–16*. London Murray.

Carpenter, T., Ansell, E., Franke, M., Fennema, E. and Weisbeck, L. (1993) 'Models of problem solving: A study of kindergarten children's problem-solving processes'. *Journal for Research in Mathematics Education*, **24**, 428–41.

Carpenter, T. and Fennema, E. (1989) 'Building on the knowledge of students and teachers' in Vergnaud, G., Rogalski, J. and Artigne, M. (eds) *Proceedings of the 13th annual conference for the Psychology of Mathematics Education*. Paris: Laboratoire de Psychologie du Development et de l'Education.

Carpenter, T. and Moser, J. (1983) 'The acquisition of addition and subtraction concepts', in R. Lesh and M. Landau (eds) *The Acquisition of Mathematics Concepts and Processes*. New York: Academic Press.

Clarke, F. and Kamii, C. (1996) 'Identification of multiplicative thinking in children in grades 1–5'. *Journal for Research in Mathematics Education*, **27**(1), 41–51.

Cobb, P., Boufi, A., McClain, K. and Whitenack, J. (1997) 'Reflective discourse and collective reflection'. *Journal for Research in Mathematics Education*, **28** (3), 258–77.

Cockcroft, W. (1982) *Mathematics Counts: Inquiry into the Teaching of Mathematics in Schools*. London: HMSO.

DES (Department of Education and Science) (1989) *Mathematics in the National Curriculum*. London: HMSO.

DFE (1995) *Mathematics in the National Curriculum*. London, HMSO.

DfEE (Department for Education and Employment) (1998) *The Implementation of the National Numeracy Strategy: Final Report of the Numeracy Task Force*. London: DfEE.

References

DfEE (Department for Education and Employment) (1999) *Framework for Teaching Mathematics from Reception to Year 6.* London: DfEE.

Dickson, L., Brown, M. and Gibson, O. (1984) *Mathematics, Teachers and Children: A Teacher's Guide to Recent Research.* London: Cassell.

Faux, G. (1998) 'For the classroom – Gattegno charts'. *Mathematics Teaching,* **163**.

Fischbein, E., Deri, M., Nello, M. and Marino, M. (1985) 'The role of implicit models in solving verbal problems in multiplication and division'. *Journal for Research in Mathematics Education,* **16**, 3–17.

Fuson, K. (1988) *Children's Counting and Concepts of Number.* New York: Springer Verlag.

Fuson, K. (1992) 'Research on whole number addition and subtraction', in D. Grouws (ed.) *Handbook of Research on Mathematics Teaching and Learning* (pp. 243–75). New York: Macmillan.

Fuson, K., Wearne, D., Hiebert, J., Murray, H., Human, P., Olivier, A., Carpenter, T. and Fennema, E. (1997) 'Children's conceptual structures for multidigit numbers and methods of multidigit addition and subtraction'. *Journal for Research in Mathematics Education,* **28** (2): 130–62.

Gelman, R. and Gallistel, C. (1978) *The Child's Understanding of Number.* Cambridge, Ma.: Harvard University Press.

Gifford, S. (1997) '"When should they start doing sums?" A critical consideration of the "emergent mathematics" approach', in I. Thompson (ed.) *Teaching and Learning Early Number.* Buckingham: Open University Press.

Ginsburg, H. (1977) *Children's Arithmetic: The Learning Process.* New York: Van Nostrand.

Gray, E. and Tall, D. (1994) 'Duality, ambiguity, and flexibility: a "Proceptual" view of simple arithmetic'. *Journal for Research in Mathematics Education,* **25**, 116–40.

Greer, B. (1992) 'Multiplication and division as models of situations', in D. Grouws *Handbook of Research on Mathematics Teaching and Learning* (pp. 276–95). New York: Macmillan.

Hart, K. (ed.) (1981) *Children's Understanding of Mathematics 11–16.* Windsor: NFER-Nelson.

Hart, K. (1989) 'There is little connection', in P. Ernest (ed.) *Mathematics Teaching: the State of the Art.* Lewes: The Falmer Press.

Hatch, G. (1998) 'Replace your mental arithmetic test with a game'. *Mathematics in School,* **27** (1), 32–5.

Holloway, K. (1997) 'Exploring mental maths', *Mathematics Teaching,* **160**, 26–9.

Huckstep, P. (1999) 'How can mathematics be useful?' *Mathematics in School,* **28** (2).

Hughes, M. (1986) *Children and Number.* Oxford: Blackwell.

Kouba, V. (1989) 'Children's solutions strategies for equivalent set multiplication and division word problems'. *Journal for Research in Mathematics Education*, **20**, 147–58.

Mcintosh, A., Reys, B. and Reys, R. (1992) 'A proposed framework for examining number sense'. *For the Learning of Mathematics*, **12** (3), 3.

Menne, J. (2000) 'Jumping ahead: an innovative teaching programme', in J. Anghileri (ed.) *Principles and Practices in Arithmetic Teaching*. Buckingham: Open University Press.

Merttens, R. (1996) *Teaching Numeracy: Mathematics in the Primary Classroom*. Leamington Spa: Scholastic.

Merttens, R. and Vass, J. (eds) (1993) *Partnership in Maths: Parents and Schools: the IMPACT project*. London: Falmer.

Moss, J. and Case, R. (1999) *Journal for Research in Mathematics Education*, **30** (2), 122–47.

Mulligan, J. and Mitchelmore, M. (1997) 'Young children's intuitive models of multiplication and division'. *Journal for Research in Mathematics Education*, **28**(3), 309–30.

Munn, P. (1994) 'The early development of literacy and numeracy skills'. *European Early Childhood Research Journal*, **2**(1), 5–18.

Munn, P. (1997) 'Children's beliefs about counting', in I. Thompson (ed.) *Teaching and Learning Early Number*. Buckingham: Open University Press.

Murray, H., Olivier, A. and Human, P. (1991) 'Young children's division strategies', in F. Furinghetti (ed.) *Proceedings of the Fifteenth International Conference for the Psychology of Mathematics Education, Vol 3* (pp. 49–56). Assissi, Italy.

NCTM (National Council for Teachers of Mathematics) (1989) *Curriculum and Evaluation Standards for School Mathematics*. Reston, Va: NCTM.

Nuffield 4 *Teacher's Handbook* (1981). Essex: Longman.

Nunes, T. and Bryant, P. (1996) *Children doing Mathematics*. Oxford: Blackwell Publishers.

Nunes, T., Schlieman, A. and Caraher, D. (1993) *Street Mathematics and School Mathematics*. New York: Cambridge University Press.

Parr, A. (1994) 'Games for playing', *Mathematics in School* **23** (3), 29–30.

Pepper, K.L. and Hunting, R.P. (1998) 'Preschoolers' counting and sharing', *Journal for Research in Mathematics Education*, **29**, 164–183.

Piaget, J. (1965) *The Child's Concept of Number*. New York: Norton.

Plunkett, S. (1979) 'Decomposition and all that rot'. *Mathematics in School*, **8**(3), 2–7.

Qualifications and Curriculum Authority (QCA) (1999) *Teaching Mental Calculation Strategies*. London: QCA.

Rousham, L. (1999) 'CAN calculators make a difference', in J. Anghileri (ed.) *Children's Mathematical Thinking in the Primary Years*. London: Cassell.

Ruthven, K. (1998) 'The use of mental, written and calculator strategies of

References

numerical computation by upper-primary pupils within a "calculator-aware" number curriculum'. *British Education Research Journal*, **24** (1).

Ruthven, K. (2000) 'The English experience of a "calculator-aware" number curriculum', in J. Anghileri (ed.) *Principles and Practices in Arithmetic Teaching*. Buckingham: Open University.

Ruthven, K. and Chaplin, D. (1998) 'The calculator as a cognitive tool'. *International Journal of Computers for Mathematics Learning*, **2**(2), 93–124.

Schaeffer, B., Eggleston, V. and Scott, J. (1974) 'Number development in young children'. *Cognitive Psychology*, **6**, 357–79.

Schlieman, A.D., Araujo, C., Cassunde, M.A., Macedo, S. and Niceas, L. (1998) 'Use of multiplicative commutativity by school children and street sellers'. *Journal for Research in Mathematics Education*, **29**(4), 422–35.

SCAA (Schools Curriculum and Assessment Authority) (1997) *Teaching and Assessment of Number in Key Stages 1 to 3*. London: SCAA.

Shuard, H., Walsh, A., Goodwin, G. and Worcester, V. (1991) *Calculators, Children and Mathematics*. London: Simon and Schuster for the National Curriculum Council.

Skemp, R. (1976) 'Relational understanding and instrumental understanding'. *Mathematics Teaching* **77**, 20–6.

Steffe, L., von Glaserfeld, E., Richard, J. and Cobb, P. (1983) *Children's Counting Types: Philosophy, Theory and Application*. New York: Praeger Scientific.

Thompson, I. (1997) 'Mental and written algorithms: can the gap be bridged?' in I. Thompson (ed.) *Teaching and Learning Early Number*. Buckingham: Open University Press.

van den Heuvel-Panhuizen, M. (2000) 'Realistic mathematics education in the Netherlands', in J. Anghileri (ed.) *Principles and Practices in Arithmetic Teaching*. Buckingham: Open University Press.

Whitebread, D. (1999) 'Emergent mathematics or how to help young children become confident mathematicians', in J. Anghileri (ed.) *Children's Mathematical Thinking in the Primary Years*. London: Cassell.

Name Index

Name Index

Subject Index

Subject Index

even number 44

factor 32, 45, 67, 69, 76, 77, 119
feedback loop 113, 137
fingers 8, 22, 29, 31, 50–3, 70, 72, 79,
    131, 133
fractions *see* decimals, fractions and
    percentages
Framework for Teaching Mathematics
    from Reception to Year 6 2, 42

games 13, 21, 29, 33, 49
Gattegno chart 11, 40
gelosia method 102–3

holistic approach 38, 95, 135

imagery 8–13, 21, 29, 31, 39, 40, 52, 60,
    80, 99, 111, 121
    see also mental imagery
instrumental understanding 7
inverse operations 54, 70, 80

language 19, 35, 37, 46, 47, 53, 57, 69,
    70, 82, 112, 115, 125, 128, 130
    difficulties 37–9

mental imagery 8–13
    resources to develop mental imagery
    29–31
    see also imagery
mental strategies 135–6
misconceptions 13, 50, 66, 76, 114,
    132–3, 136, 137
multiplication and division 67–88
    commutative rule 74–6
    diversity in meanings 72
    division with larger numbers 84–8
    early experiences 69–70
    introducing the symbols 73–4, 76
    inverse operations 70–1
    learning the facts 77–80
    mental strategies for multiplying
    larger numbers 82–4
    multiples and powers of ten 80–2
    number patterns 70, 71–2
    remainders 71

National Numeracy Strategy *see*
    Framework for Teaching
    Mathematics from Reception to
    Year 6

'nice' number 32
number bonds 29, 42, 43, 52, 61
number line 10, 13, 29–31, 36, 40, 48,
    50, 110–11, 115–16
    see also empty number line
number patterns 3, 4, 8, 22–5, 28, 32,
    44–5, 47, 70–2, 77–9, 110
number triples 54, 55, 76
numerator 115, 119

one-to-one correspondence 18, 23, 25,
    27
order-irrelevance principle 27
ordinal (aspect of number) 17, 18, 22,
    25

partial sum approach 95
partitioning numbers 5, 37–8, 61, 63,
    94–5, 101
partitive division 69
pattern recognition 18, 22, 24
percentages *see* decimals, fractions and
    percentages
place value 9, 10, 13, 25, 30, 35–40, 63,
    82, 92–8, 101, 112
prime number 32, 45
procept 33–5, 42, 56, 70
purposes in teaching mathematics
    15–16

Qualifications and Curriculum
    Authority (QCA) 110
quotitive division 69

rational number 5, 110
recording *see* written calculations
rectangular array 67
relational understanding 7
remainders 71, 123

scale factor 67, 69, 76
Schools Curriculum and Assessment
    Authority (SCAA) 25, 36, 38
sequence methods 62–5
skip counting 71
split tens methods 62–4, 92, 94, 95
square number 45
subitizing 23
subtraction *see* addition and
    subtraction

symbols
    for numbers 33–7
    for operations 40–3

148